MONTANA WILDLIFE VIEWING GUIDE

Carol and Hank Fischer

FALCON

Helena, Montana

Author
Carol and Hank Fischer

Illustrations
Leslie LeRoux

Front Cover Photo
Grizzly bear, DONALD M. JONES

Back Cover Photos
Reynolds Mountain, Glacier National Park, DARRIN SCHREDER
Western Tanager, DONALD M. JONES

Copyright © 1995 by Falcon Press Publishing Co., Inc.,
Helena and Billings, Montana.
Published in cooperation with Defenders of Wildlife.

Defenders of Wildlife and its design are registered
marks of Defenders of Wildlife, Washington, D.C.

Watchable Wildlife is a registered trademark of Falcon Press Publishing Co., Inc.

Design, typesetting, and other prepress work by Falcon Press,
Helena, Montana.

Printed in Malaysia
ISBN 1-56044-348-0

Library of Congress Cataloging-in-Publication Data

Fischer, Carol.
   Montana wildlife viewing guide / Carol and Hank Fischer.
      p. cm. — (Watchable wildlife series)
   Includes index.
   ISBN 1-56044-348-0
   1. Wildlife viewing sites—Montana—Guidebooks. 2. Wildlife
watching–Montana–Guidebooks. 3. Montana—Guidebooks.
I. Fischer, Hank. II. Title. III. Series.
   QL188.F57 1995
   599-09786—dc20   95-10265
                                                    CIP

CONTENTS

PROJECT SPONSORS

 DEFENDERS OF WILDLIFE is a national nonprofit organization of more than 80,000 members and supporters dedicated to preserving the natural abundance and diversity of wildlife and its habitat. A one-year membership is $20 and includes six issues of *Defenders*, an award-winning conservation magazine, and *Wildlife Advocate*, an activist-oriented newsletter. To join or for further information, write or call Defenders of Wildlife, 1101 14th Street NW, Suite 1400, Washington, DC 20005, (202) 682-9400.

 The USDA FOREST SERVICE has a mandate to protect, improve, and wisely use the nation's forest and range resources for multiple purposes for the benefit of all Americans. The 10 national forests of Montana are sponsors of this program to promote awareness and enjoyment of fish and wildlife on our national forest lands. USDA Forest Service, Northern Region, Federal Building, 200 East Broadway, P.O. Box 7669, Missoula, MT 59807, (406) 329-3511.

 The BUREAU OF LAND MANAGEMENT is responsible for the management of more than 8 million acres of public lands, their resources and values in Montana, to best serve the needs of the American people. The goals of multiple-use management is to sustain the integrity, diversity, and productivity of ecological systems while providing the goods and services for present and future generations. BLM's Watchable Wildlife program fosters public awareness and appreciation of vast biological, recreational, and educational opportunities offered by America's public lands. For more information, contact the Bureau of Land Management, P.O. Box 36800, Billings, MT 59107-6800, (406) 255-2938.

 The U.S. FISH & WILDLIFE SERVICE programs include the national wildlife refuge system, protection of threatened and endangered species, conservation of migratory birds, fisheries restoration, recreation and education, wildlife research, and law enforcement. The USFWS administers 1.1 million acres in Montana that include 20 wildlife refuges, 10 waterfowl production areas, and 3 fish hatcheries. Its mission is to conserve, protect, and enhance fish and wildlife and their habitats for the continuing benefit of the American people. Contact U.S. Fish & Wildlife Service, Contact U.S. Fish & Wildlife Service, Refuges and Wildlife, P.O. Box 25486, Denver, CO 80225, (303) 236-8145.

 The BUREAU OF RECLAMATION manages and develops water and related resources to conserve and, where appropriate, to enhance fish and wildlife habitat and populations. In Montana, a dozen major Reclamation reservoirs provide supplemental water to a diverse user group, from irrigation districts to municipalities, as well as state and federal wildlife refuges. Contact Bureau of Reclamation, P.O. Box 30137, Billings, MT 59107-0137, (406) 657-6688.

 The NATIONAL PARK SERVICE manages 1.2 million acres in Montana, including two national parks, one national monument, on national battlefield, one national recreation area, and two national historic sites. The NPS was established to conserve and protect resources umimpaired for future generations while providing for public use and enjoyment. Contact Glacier National Park, West Glacier, MT 59936, (406) 888-5441; Yellowstone National Park, P.O. Box 168, Yellowstone National Park, WY 82190, (307) 344-7381.

MONTANA FISH, WILDLIFE & PARKS manages more than 490,000 acres, including 41 state parks, 65 wildlife management areas, and over 300 fishing access sites. The land managed by FWP is dispersed throughout the state. FWP is charged with the responsibility for managing Montana's fish, wildlife, and recreational resources, and for providing optimum outdoor recreational opportunities for Montanans and visitors. Contact Montana Fish, Wildlife & Parks, P.O. Box 200701, 1420 East Sixth Avenue, Helena, MT 59620, (406) 444-1276.

The MONTANA DEPARTMENT OF STATE LANDS owns 1.5 million acres in Montana (5.5 percent of Montana lands). Approximately two-thirds of the land is east of the Continental Divide. The state was originally granted two sections in each township in its enabling legislation to support public schools. Many of these sections have since been traded to gain larger blocks of state lands. The DSL has four major missions: trust land management, wildlife suppression, mined land reclamation, and forestry assistance. Contact Montana Department of State Lands, 1625 11th Avenue, P.O. Box 201601, Helena, MT 59620, (406) 444-4560.

TRAVEL MONTANA, MONTANA DEPARTMENT OF COMMERCE. Travel Montana's mission is to strengthen Montana's economy through the promotion of the state as a vacation destination and film location. By maximizing the combined talents and abilities of its staff, and with guidance from the Governor's Tourism Advisory Council, Travel Montana strives to promote a quality experience to visitors while encouraging preservation of Montana's environment and quality of life. Contact Travel Montana, Montana Dept. of Commerce, 1424 Ninth Avenue, Helena, MT 59620, (406) 444-2654.

The MONTANA STATE PARKS AND WILDLIFE INTERPRETIVE ASSOCIATION is a nonprofit organization that promotes interpretive, historical, scientific, and educational activities of the Montana Department of Fish, Wildlife and Parks, and assists in the development and improvement of interpretive materials and facilities. The association recognizes the diverse public interest in the state's natural resources and seeks to implement interpretive programs consistent with those interests. Contact Montana State Parks and Wildlife Interpretive Association,

The MONTANA AUDUBON COUNCIL is the umbrella organization for Montana's 9 chapters of the National Audubon Society: Flathead Basin, Missoula, Bitterroot Valley, Great Falls, Helena, Butte-Dillon, Bozeman, Billings, and Miles City. With a collective membership of 2,400, MAC works to preserve the integrity of Montana's natural communities and functioning ecosystems with a committment to activism and education. Contact Montana Audubon Council, State Office, P.O. Box 595, Helena, MT 59624, (406) 443-3949.

OTHER IMPORTANT CONTRIBUTORS

The Nature Conservancy
Patagonia, Inc.
Len and Sandy Sargent
Bob and Hopie Stevens

INTRODUCTION

From alpine meadows and glacial lakes to rugged badlands and shortgrass prairies, few states can match the spectacular diversity of wildlife found in Montana. In all, more than 500 species of mammals, birds, reptiles, and amphibians may be found in the Big Sky State. Consider just a few of Montana's wildlife viewing superlatives:

• The largest breeding population of trumpeter swans in the lower U.S.
• It claims the site where more golden eagles have been seen in a single day than anywhere else in the country.
• The largest population of nesting common loons in the western United States.
• The largest native herd of Rocky Mountain bighorn sheep in the U.S.
• The largest grizzly bear population south of Canada.
• The largest population of gray wolves west of the Mississippi.

No single book could ever include all of the wildlife viewing opportunities in Montana. This revised edition contains only a sampling of the very best sites. In preparing for the revision, the authors, working with a committee of wildlife and land management experts, reviewed the original volume. Several viewing areas were dropped, and new sites added. Site descriptions and directions were checked and updated. New interpretive artwork appears on pages 14-21. Also included in this revision is an index of popular wildlife species, keyed to the best sites for viewing them.

Use this guide to observe, and learn more about wildlife species. Use it to plan trips to one or more specific viewing areas, or to augment a trip taken for another purpose. Support wildlife conservation efforts in Montana and elsewhere. Above all, savor your wildlife discoveries and the memories you make.

THE NATIONAL WATCHABLE WILDLIFE PROGRAM

State wildlife programs historically were funded through license fees for hunting and fishing, and by federal taxes on guns, ammunition, and fishing tackle. These funds were used to enhance and preserve wildlife habitat, benefitting game and nongame species alike. Today, however, these revenues are declining and cannot meet the escalating cost of wildlife management programs and threats to wildlife habitat.

As participation in hunting has declined, public interest in wildlife viewing and related recreation has increased dramatically. In Montana, wildlife-related activities other than hunting and fishing generated an estimated 104 million dollars in 1991. Nationally, more than 76 million people aged 16 or older participated in some form of wildlife viewing activity in 1991.

The National Watchable Wildlife Program was initiated in response to this growing interest in viewing native, free-roaming wildlife in its natural habitat. Eight federal land management agencies, the International Association of Fish and Wildlife Agencies, and four national conservation groups agreed in 1990 to develop wildlife viewing opportunities, and to heighten public awareness of wildlife and conservation issues.

Montana was among the first states to publish a wildlife viewing guide and promote a statewide network of wildlife viewing areas. Since its release in 1990, 22 other states have followed suit. At the time this book was revised in January of 1995, at least 10 more states were developing or considering a viewing guide project. The goal of Watchable Wildlife, a national network of wildlife viewing sites linked by the brown-and-white binoculars sign, soon may be within reach.

TIPS FOR VIEWING WILDLIFE

Much of the excitement of wildlife viewing stems from the fact that you can never be sure of what you will see. While many species are difficult to view under the best of circumstances, there are several things you can do to greatly increase your chances of seeing wild animals in their natural environs.

The cardinal rule of wildlife viewing is patience. If you arrive at a viewing site expecting to see every species noted in this guide on your first visit, you surely will be disappointed. Review the tips below, and enjoy your time in the outdoors, regardless of what you see.

Prepare for your outing. Some of the viewing sites in this guide are remote and have no facilities. Review each site account before you visit, checking for warnings about services and road conditions. Always carry water, even in winter. Dress appropriately for the area and season. Detailed maps of many featured areas may be obtained through the U.S. Forest Service, Bureau of Land Management, Montana Department of State Lands, or other public agencies. Always travel with an up-to-date road atlas.

Visit when animals are active. The single most important way to increase your chances of seeing wildlife is to arrive early—right at dawn. This is nearly always the best time for viewing, with dusk a close second. A wildlife viewing trip during the heat of a summer day is usually a prescription for disappointment.

Wildlife viewing is often seasonal. Many wildlife species are present only during certain times of year. Waterfowl and shorebirds are best viewed when they migrate through Montana in large numbers. Bald eagles may be seen year-round, but their numbers increase dramatically during the fall migration period. Each site description in this guide contains a wealth of information about optimal viewing seasons for selected species. Consult a field guide for additional information, or contact the site manager for an update before you visit.

Use field guides. Pocket field guides are essential for positive identification of the many animals named at each viewing site. Guides are available for virtually every plant and animal found in Montana, and contain valuable information about where animals live, what they eat, and how they rear their young.

Use binoculars or a spotting scope. Viewing aids bridge the distance between you and wild animals. Binoculars come in different sizes such as 7 x 35, 8 x 40, and 10 x 50. The first number in the pair refers to how large the animal will be magnified compared to the naked eye. The second number refers to the diameter of the lens that faces the animal. The larger that number, the greater the amount of light entering the lens—which means better viewing in dim light.

Move slowly and quietly. When you arrive at a viewing site, you can employ several strategies for observing wildlife. You can stay in your vehicle and wait for animals to pass by. You can find a comfortable place, sit down, and remain still. Or you can quietly walk in search of wildlife. Take a few steps, stop, look, and listen. Use your ears to locate birds or the movements of other animals. Walk into the wind if possible, avoiding brittle sticks or leaves. Use trees and vegetation as a blind. Wear dark-colored clothes or camouflage. Consider using a dropcloth of camouflage netting or a portable blind.

Enjoy wildlife at a distance. You can actually harm the wildlife you care about by getting too close. Move away from an animal that stops feeding and raises its head sharply, appears nervous, stands up suddenly, or changes its direction of travel. Causing an animal to change its behavior is harassment. In national parks, you can be fined for harassing or approaching wildlife too closely. Leave pets at home—domestic animals may chase or kill wildlife, putting the wildlife, or even you, in danger.

Never touch orphaned or sick animals. Young wild animals that appear to be alone usually have parents waiting nearby. If you believe an animal is injured, sick, or abandoned, contact the site owner or the nearest wildlife agency.

Some wildlife can be dangerous. Do not approach bears, and remember that sow bears with cubs can be extremely dangerous. Rutting bull elk in the fall, cow moose with calves, and bison can all be very dangerous and should never be approached. Rattlesnakes inhabit some of the drier, rockier areas of Montana; be alert for snakes as you hike in these areas.

Honor the rights of private landowners. A few of the sites in this guide feature roadside viewing adjacent to private lands. Always get permission before entering private property.

Responsible wildlife viewing means not interfering with the normal behavior of animals. In the scene above, a bull elk passes near a photographer. While this person remains close to his car—a wise move—he unwittingly has blocked the elk's preferred direction of travel.
NEAL AND MARY JANE MISHLER

Honor the rights of other wildlife viewers. Keep voices low. If many people are viewing, please be patient and allow others to enjoy a quality experience. Leave wildlife habitat in better condition than you found it. Pick up litter and dispose of it properly.

HOW TO USE THIS GUIDE

Montana is divided into 6 **travel regions** shown on the state map, pages 12-13. Each region, along with Montana's two national parks, forms a separate chapter of this book. A **full-color map** opens each region, identifying all viewing sites by number, along with major towns and roads. **Tabs** featuring the name of each region appear on page margins, allowing the reader to move quickly from one region to the next.

Each wildlife **viewing site** contains a **description** of the area, including major habitat types and physiographic features, information on major wildlife species, and optimal seasons or months for viewing them. Also included in the description are notes on access and seasonal closures. *NOTES OF CAUTION REGARDING ROAD CONDITIONS, VIEWING LIMITATIONS, AND OTHER RESTRICTIONS APPEAR IN CAPITAL LETTERS.*

Written **directions** to each site appear beneath the site description. **Site maps** are also included for a few viewing sites with difficult access. Please supplement all directions in this guide with an up-to-date state or county road atlas. The **agency name** and **phone number** of the **site owner/manager** appears at the bottom of the site account; use this phone number to obtain additional information about viewing opportunities, road conditions, etc. The name of the **closest town** offering gas and a telephone is also included.

Beneath the written information is a list of **facility icons.** These symbols provide valuable information about entrance fees, recreational opportunities, and barrier-free access. *PLEASE CONTACT THE SITE MANAGER FOR ADDITIONAL INFORMATION REGARDING BARRIER-FREE ACCESS.* In most cases, viewing sites offering barrier-free access include accessible restrooms and parking, and some portion of the viewing area.

SITE OWNER/MANAGER ABBREVIATIONS

USFWS: U.S. Fish and Wildlife Service
FWP: Montana Fish, Wildlife & Parks
USFS: USDA Forest Service
BLM: Bureau of Land Management
NPS: National Park Service
ACE: U.S. Army Corps of Engineers
DNR: Montana Department of Natural Resources
MSL: Montana State Lands
PVT: Private Ownership
BOR: Bureau of Reclamation

MONTANA
wildlife viewing areas

Montana is divided into six travel regions and two national parks shown on this map.
Each region and national park forms a separate chapter of this guide. A detailed
regional map appears at the start of each chapter.

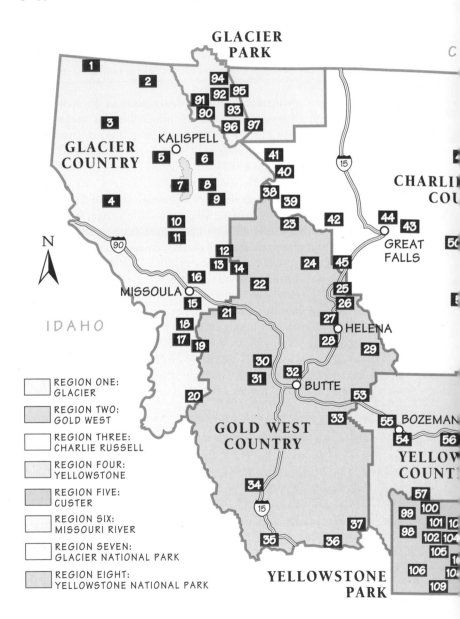

GLACIER
PARK

1

2

94
92 95
91 93
90
96 97

3

GLACIER
COUNTRY

KALISPELL

5   6

7   8
9

4

41
40

38
39

10
11

23

42

44 43

56

GREAT
FALLS

12
13 14

24

45

25
26

22

16

MISSOULA

15

21

27

28

HELENA

29

18
17 19

30
31

32

BUTTE

53

20

33

55 BOZEMAN

54   56

34

37

36

35

GOLD WEST
COUNTRY

YELLOWSTONE
PARK

CHARLI
COU

15

90

N

IDAHO

YELLOW
COUNT

57
99 100
101 10
98 102 104
105
106   10
109

REGION ONE:
GLACIER

REGION TWO:
GOLD WEST

REGION THREE:
CHARLIE RUSSELL

REGION FOUR:
YELLOWSTONE

REGION FIVE:
CUSTER

REGION SIX:
MISSOURI RIVER

REGION SEVEN:
GLACIER NATIONAL PARK

REGION EIGHT:
YELLOWSTONE NATIONAL PARK

FACILITIES AND RECREATION ICONS

 Parking

 Entry Fee

 Restrooms

 Handicapped Accessible

 Picnic

 Restaurant

 Lodging

Camping

Hiking

Cross-country Skiing

Bicycling

Boat Ramp

Large Boats

Small Boats

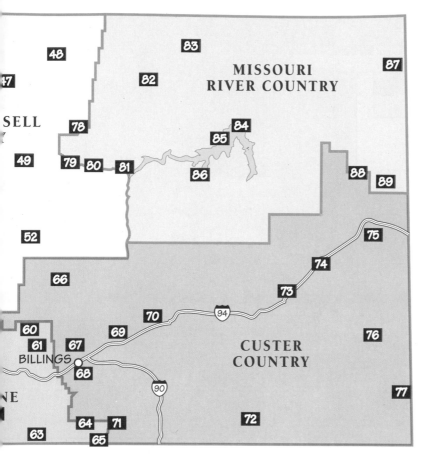

D A

48

47

SELL

78

49

79 80 81

52

66

60

61 67

BILLINGS

68

NE

64 71

63

65

83

82

MISSOURI
RIVER COUNTRY

85 84

86

87

88

89

75

74

73

70 94

69

76

CUSTER
COUNTRY

77

90

72

HIGHWAY SIGNS

As you travel in Montana and other states, look for these signs on interstates, highways, and other roads. They identify the route to follow to reach wildlife viewing sites.

13

Coniferous Forest

NORTHERN GOSHAWK

LODGEPOLE PINE

PINE MARTEN

PONDEROSA PINE

SUBALPINE FIR

ELK

MULE DEER

BLACK BEAR

CECROPIA MOTH

ALLIGATOR LIZARD (NORTHERN)

SHOOTING STAR

HARLEQUIN DUCK

LUPINE

This forested habitat, which covers approximately 30 percent of the state, is associated primarily with mountains and is most common in western Montana.

Different types of conifers support different species of wildlife. The western tanager, red-naped sapsucker, and yellow-rumped warbler live in old growth Douglas-fir forests. Dense lodgepole pine forests supply the Cassin's finch and pine siskin with seeds from pine cones; blue grouse actually digest the resin-soaked needles from these trees. Deer and elk can escape from predators here.

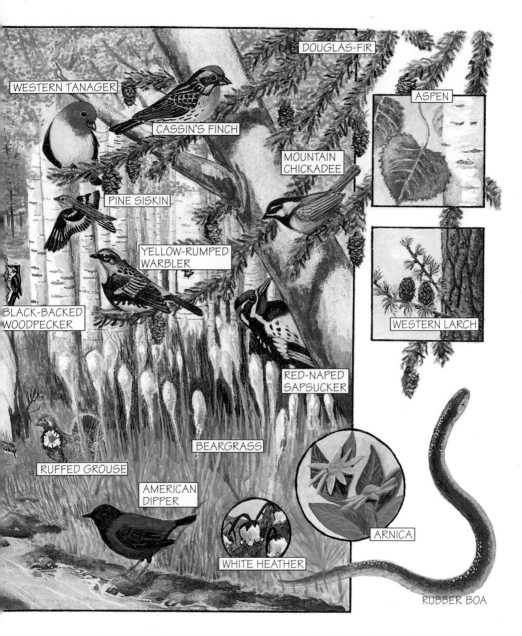

DOUGLAS-FIR

WESTERN TANAGER

CASSIN'S FINCH

MOUNTAIN CHICKADEE

ASPEN

PINE SISKIN

YELLOW-RUMPED WARBLER

WESTERN LARCH

BLACK-BACKED WOODPECKER

RED-NAPED SAPSUCKER

BEARGRASS

RUFFED GROUSE

AMERICAN DIPPER

ARNICA

WHITE HEATHER

RUBBER BOA

Even after a tree is dead, it continues to provide habitat and nourishment for wildlife. Decaying logs on the forest floor supply homes for insects, which in turn become nourishment for bears and other wildlife. Standing dead trees, known as *snags*, provide shelter, nesting space, and hunting perches for mammals, birds, and insects.

Lowland River Forest

TIGER SWALLOWTAIL

GREEN ASH

WILD ROSE

MOCK-ORANGE

DAMSELFLY

BLACK-HEADED GROSBEAK

OSPREY

AMERICAN REDSTART

YELLOW WARBLER

PILEATED WOODPECKER

ALDER

COMMON MERGANSER

SPOTTED SANDPIPER

RIVER OTTER

WESTSLOPE CUTTHROAT TRO

LLDW 94

Look along the banks of most Montana streams and rivers and you'll see a narrow band of shrubs and deciduous trees, called a *riparian zone*. This streamside habitat accounts for less than 1 percent of all land in Montana—but it supports more than half of the state's wildlife species! In some areas, the riparian zone provides the only shelter for miles around.

Riparian zones are often places where several different habitats meet: grassy uplands, brushy beaver ponds and river banks, marshy sloughs, and thick timber. These "edge areas" are often the best places to see wildlife.

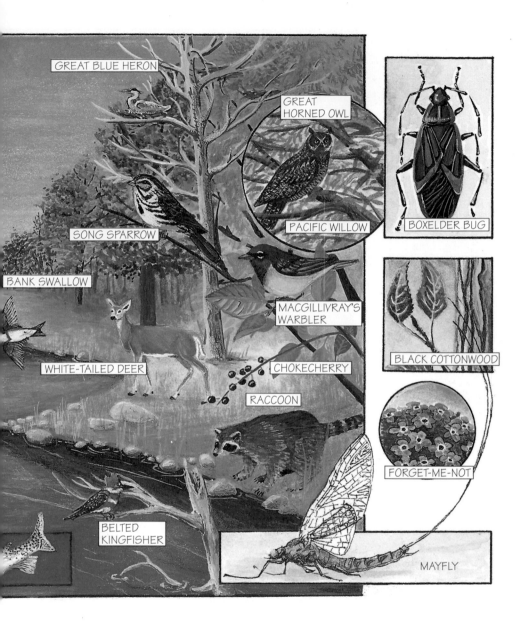

GREAT BLUE HERON

GREAT
HORNED OWL

SONG SPARROW

PACIFIC WILLOW

BOXELDER BUG

BANK SWALLOW

MACGILLIVRAY'S
WARBLER

BLACK COTTONWOOD

WHITE-TAILED DEER

CHOKECHERRY

RACCOON

FORGET-ME-NOT

BELTED
KINGFISHER

MAYFLY

Streamside forests tend to support more insects than surrounding habitats, which in turn attract insect-eating songbirds and bats. Pileated woodpeckers, great horned owls, and squirrels make their nests in the standing dead trees near streams and rivers. The branches of these forests are ideal for nesting colonies, or *rookeries*, of great blue herons.

Inland Marsh

NORTHERN HARRIER

SHORT-EARED OWL

LONG-TAILED WEASEL

MOURNING CLOAK BUTTERFLY

WESTERN TERRESTRIAL GARTER SNAKE

YELLOW-HEADED BLACKBIRD

CATTAIL

MUSKRAT

NORTHERN PINTAIL

RUDDY DUCK

DAMSELFLY

A *marsh* is a body of standing water with plants growing in it. Marshes comprise less than 1 percent of the land area of Montana. Cattails, bullrushes, and grasses often thrive along the shore. Reeds and water lilies float on the surface. In late summer, algae blooms in the water create a sweet smell of decomposition.

COMMON YELLOWTHROAT

TAILED FROG

MEADOW VOLE

TUNDRA SWAN

RED-WINGED BLACKBIRD

MARSH WREN

WATER LILY

PAINTED TURTLE

Muskrats feed on cattail stems, while waterfowl take advantage of the open water created by the muskrats. Waterfowl, insects, and amphibians such as frogs and salamanders breed here. Preying on nests of waterfowl along the marsh's edge are coyotes, foxes, and raccoons. The osprey, northern harrier, and short-eared owl hunt from the sky.

Prairie Grassland

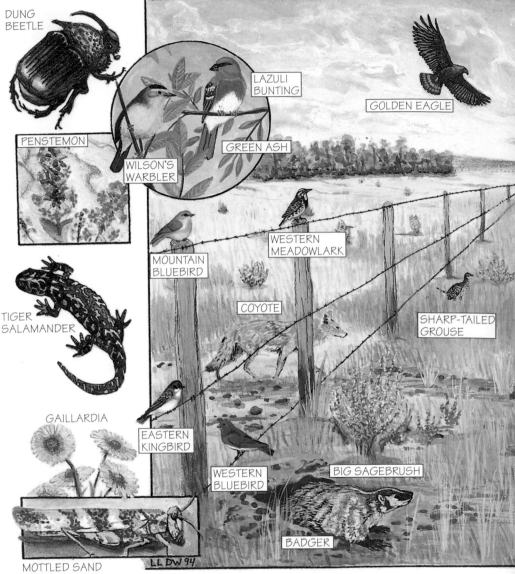

DUNG BEETLE

LAZULI BUNTING

GOLDEN EAGLE

PENSTEMON

WILSON'S WARBLER

GREEN ASH

WESTERN MEADOWLARK

MOUNTAIN BLUEBIRD

TIGER SALAMANDER

COYOTE

SHARP-TAILED GROUSE

GAILLARDIA

EASTERN KINGBIRD

WESTERN BLUEBIRD

BIG SAGEBRUSH

BADGER

MOTTLED SAND GRASSHOPPER

LL DW 94

Flat or rolling prairies contain grasses, flowers, shrubs, and occasional trees. The prairie grassland endures scorching heat, hollowing winds, and long, cold winters. More than 65 percent of Montana consists of this type of habitat, with the great majority of it located east of the Continental Divide.

A prairie dog town is one of the best places to see the interrelationship of wildlife in a prairie grassland habitat. Prairie dog burrows become homes for ground squirrels,

WOOD NYMPH

FERRUGINOUS HAWK

SHRUBBY
EVENING
PRIMROSE

BLACK-BILLED
MAGPIE

PRONGHORN

SILVER-SPOTTED
SKIPPER

WHITE-TAILED
JACKRABBIT

BLACK-TAILED
PRAIRIE DOG

PACIFIC
KANGAROO RAT

RATTLESNAKE
(WESTERN)

SAVANNAH
SPARROW

BURROWING OWL

burrowing owls, white-tailed jackrabbits, and many other smaller species. Savannah
and vesper sparrows, mountain plovers, and western meadowlarks nest on the ground.
Sharp-tailed grouse use the heavily-grazed open areas as dancing grounds to attract
mates. On the edges of the town, pronghorn, mule deer, and elk graze the vigorous
grasses stimulated by the light grazing of prairie dogs. Farther out, coyotes, bobcats,
and badgers wait for their chance to grab a meal, while eagles and hawks circle overhead .

REGION ONE: GLACIER COUNTRY

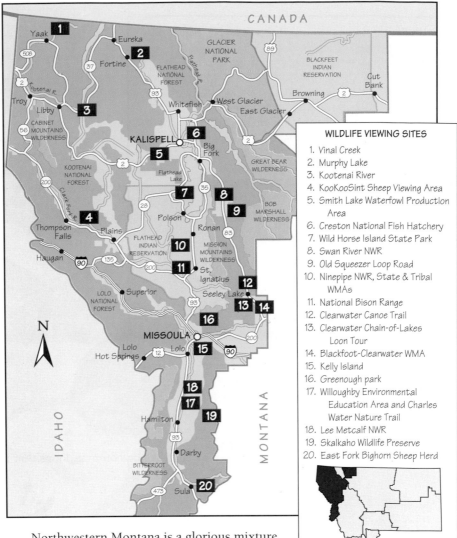

WILDLIFE VIEWING SITES

1. Vinal Creek
2. Murphy Lake
3. Kootenai River
4. KooKooSint Sheep Viewing Area
5. Smith Lake Waterfowl Production Area
6. Creston National Fish Hatchery
7. Wild Horse Island State Park
8. Swan River NWR
9. Old Squeezer Loop Road
10. Ninepipe NWR, State & Tribal WMAs
11. National Bison Range
12. Clearwater Canoe Trail
13. Clearwater Chain-of-Lakes Loon Tour
14. Blackfoot-Clearwater WMA
15. Kelly Island
16. Greenough park
17. Willoughby Environmental Education Area and Charles Water Nature Trail
18. Lee Metcalf NWR
19. Skalkaho Wildlife Preserve
20. East Fork Bighorn Sheep Herd

Northwestern Montana is a glorious mixture of dense pine forests, craggy peaks, and clear, rushing rivers. The most famous place is Glacier National Park, home to mountain goats, bighorn sheep, and the largest population of grizzly bears in the lower 48 states. Glacier's recently-established gray wolf population is another source of high visitor interest. This region is also notable for its glacial lakes and prairie potholes. Ninepipe National Wildlife Refuge, with its picture-perfect Mission Mountains backdrop, offers terrific birding for waterfowl, shorebirds, and raptors. Wild Horse Island in Flathead Lake offers unparalleled opportunities to see bighorn sheep and bald eagles in pristine surroundings. The Skalkaho Wildlife Preserve offers excellent wildlife viewing from a mountain bike; visitors can almost always hear bull elk bugling in the fall. On the unique Clearwater Canoe Trail, look for common loons, wood ducks, and ever-abundant turtles.

1. VINAL CREEK

Description: Moist, coastal weather in this part of the Kootenai National Forest has created impressive old-growth forests. The first 3 miles of this trail along Vinal Creek pass through a stand of western larch, with some trees 4 feet or more in diameter and most over 300 years old. At the creek crossing, there are huge red cedars, some more than 25 feet around, providing habitat for pileated woodpeckers, barred owls, goshawks, and numerous warblers, vireos, and kinglets. The trail splits near the 28-foot Turner Falls; the uphill fork goes to Mount Henry, while the other leads to a chain of 5 lakes (Fish Lakes) in a narrow canyon. Along the Fish Lakes Trail (#397), look for deer and moose. The rocky canyon is a good place to see and hear pikas. Waterfowl such as common or Barrow's goldeneyes can be seen in the lakes; common loons and great blue herons are sometimes spotted, too. Watch for belted kingfishers and American dippers along streamside areas. The fairly level trail is good for cross-country skiing and viewing deer and elk in the winter. *FOREST ROAD 746 IS TYPICALLY PLOWED ONLY TO WITHIN 1 MILE OF TRAILHEAD.*

Directions: *From U.S. Highway 2, follow Secondary Route 508 to Yaak. Take Forest Road 68 for 3 miles, then follow Forest Road 746 for 5 miles (this road parallels the east side of the upper Yaak River). The well-marked trail begins just north of a bridge that crosses Vinal Creek.*

Ownership: USFS (406) 293-6211
Size: 6-mile trail   **Closest Town:** Yaak

2. MURPHY LAKE

Description: This small lake is in a heavily forested area with adjacent marshland. Interpretive signs at the picnic area describe the common loons that nest here and their habitat. Nesting loons are very sensitive, and signed buoys mark areas closed to the public. Visitors may pick up a brochure at the trailhead and hike the moderate 1-mile trail to an observation deck. Birders may see common loons, horned grebes, waterfowl, bald eagles, and osprey. Beavers can also be seen. Much of the land north of Murphy Lake is key winter range for white-tailed and mule deer. A cross-country ski trail marked by signs goes just east of Murphy Lake off Forest Road 7008 and passes through this range, where moose are also occasionally spotted.

Directions: *From Eureka, follow U.S. Highway 93 for 14 miles southeast, then take Forest Road 7008 at the northwest corner of Murphy Lake. Follow this road to the picnic area, loon information signs, and trailhead.*

Ownership: USFS (406) 882-4451
Size: 200 acres   **Closest Town:** Eureka

3. KOOTENAI RIVER

Description: The Kootenai is a beautiful, large mountain river and an outstanding site for viewing bald eagles, nesting osprey, great blue herons, and waterfowl. On the east bank of the David Thompson Bridge just below the powerhouse, watch bald eagles and osprey diving for fish and returning to nearby snags; there are more than 20 nests between Libby and the dam. In the fall, bald eagles concentrate below the dam to catch kokanee salmon. Over 160 bald eagles have been sighted in a day. Eagle migration starts in October, peaks in the middle of November, and tapers off near the end of December. In March, large waterfowl concentrations pass through. The U.S. Army Corps of Engineers has placed goose nesting platforms on the river between the dam and the Montana Highway 37 bridge. A river float between Libby Dam and the town of Libby is an excellent way to view raptors and waterfowl. Wildlife viewers can continue along the Kootenai River by driving west on U.S. Highway 2 from Libby to Kootenai Falls. Watch for bighorn sheep on the north side of the river and harlequin ducks breeding at Kootenai Falls during April and May. Two wildlife interpretive exhibits can be found along this stretch. Floaters can launch a boat at the Alexander Creek Recreation Area and take out at the old bridge abutments, about 8 miles downriver from the dam, or at Libby, 17 miles downriver.

Directions: *From Libby, take Montana Highway 37 for 16 miles to the Jennings Hi-line Road, and turn left. Follow this road to the David Thompson Bridge. View from the designated viewing areas or from the sidewalks on the bridge. From Libby, drive west 10 miles along U.S. Highway 2 to Kootenai Falls.*

Ownership: PVT, USFS, ACE (406) 293-5577
Size: 27-mile stretch   **Closest Town:** Libby

4. KOOKOOSINT SHEEP VIEWING AREA

Description: Flanked by rocky outcroppings, this small meadow often provides opportunities to view bighorn sheep within 50 feet of a road—sometimes in herds of up to 100. There are wildlife information signs at the site. The best time to view sheep is October 15 through May 1, with peak viewing during breeding season, November 15 through December 31. Bighorns may be seen anywhere along Montana Highway 200 for about 7 miles on either side of this area. A few miles to the west on an island close to where the Clark Fork and Thompson Rivers join, look for elk during the spring and osprey, great blue herons, and waterfowl during the summer.

Directions: *From Thompson Falls, drive 8 miles east on Montana Highway 200.*

Ownership: PVT, State of MT, USFS (406) 826-3821
Size: 0.25 acre   **Closest Town:** Thompson Falls

5. SMITH LAKE WATERFOWL PRODUCTION AREA

Description: *URBAN SITE.* This large waterfowl area with extensive marshes and a significant lake is a good area for viewing shorebirds such as phalaropes, yellowlegs, and killdeer. Look for waterfowl such as mallard, American wigeon, pintail, and gadwall, as well as nesting Canada geese, grebes, and assorted gulls. Other species of special interest include tundra swans in late March and early April, and American bitterns. In spring and fall, look for sandhill cranes in the western grassy meadows. Watch for bluebirds along the road on the way in. Smith Lake and Ashley Creek are open year-round to boating—a good way to view the varied wildlife. *UPLAND AREAS CLOSED MARCH 1 THROUGH JULY 1.*

Directions: *From Kalispell, follow U.S. Highway 2 west for 7 miles to Big Horn Drive. Turn south, then take Smith Lake Road to the Kila Fishing Access.*

Ownership: FWP, USFWS (406) 755-4375
Size: 1,040 acres   **Closest Town:** Kalispell

A young bighorn ram rubs the face of an elder during a social visit. Bighorn sheep provide excellent viewing opportunities at several sites, including the KooKooSint Viewing Area near Thompson Falls (see opposite page). RALEIGH MEADE

6. CRESTON NATIONAL FISH HATCHERY

Description: Situated along a beautiful spring creek, this hatchery raises rainbow, cutthroat, and bull trout, and kokanee salmon. At its peak, it holds over 2 million fish. The raceways immediately adjacent to the buildings are open for public viewing. The building where spawning occurs has displays explaining how fish eggs are fertilized, how they develop, and how they hatch. Watch the kokanee salmon spawning procedures between early November and the end of January. The hatchery reaches maximum fish populations between April and June. Many fish-eating birds, including osprey, great blue herons, belted kingfishers, and magpies can be seen in the vicinity. The pond and picnic area across the road from the hatchery almost always have several Canada geese broods in the summer. The hatchery is open daily, 7:30 a.m. - 4 p.m.

Directions: *From Big Fork, take Montana Highway 35 north towards Creston and follow for about 9 miles. Just east of Creston, take Creston Hatchery Road and drive about 1 mile to the hatchery.*

Ownership: USFWS (406) 755-7870
Size: 74 acres   **Closest Town:** Creston

7. WILD HORSE ISLAND STATE PARK

Description: A largely undeveloped island in Flathead Lake with flower-covered uplands and forested slopes, Wild Horse Island is the largest island in the largest freshwater lake west of Minnesota. Look in the high rocky area in the island's northwest corner for a herd of about 100 bighorn sheep. Also look for nesting bald eagles, waterfowl, osprey, goshawks, mule deer, coyotes, marmots, numerous songbirds—and a few remaining wild horses. To preserve the island's natural features, there are no visitor facilities or public docks, so boats must be beached. There are 54 private lots on the island; please respect the owners' rights. Hiking is possible on the numerous wildlife trails.

Directions: *Take U.S. Highway 93 to Polson. Island visitors can either take a tour boat from Polson or rent a boat in Big Arm along the west side of the lake. Public boat launch at Big Arm.*

Ownership: FWP (406) 752-5501
Size: 2,165 acres   **Closest Town:** Polson

8. SWAN RIVER NATIONAL WILDLIFE REFUGE

Description: This undisturbed and undeveloped refuge contains extensive swampland and coniferous forest. The refuge is home to elk, deer, moose, grizzly bears, and black bears. Its 171 bird species include bald eagles, great blue herons, and black terns. A walk along Bog Road or a Swan River canoe trip are both excellent for birding. In the spring watch for tundra swans, nesting bald eagles, bobolinks, and northern harriers. In the summer look for wood ducks and yellowlegs. An eastern phoebe has been sighted here, a rare occurrence in Montana. The Flathead Audubon Society has adopted this refuge and plans to build an observation platform. A canoe trip on the Swan River is the best way to see the refuge. Put in at the first county bridge upstream from Swan Lake off Porcupine Road; it's an easy 3- to 4-mile float. To take out, paddle across Swan Lake to a Forest Service boat ramp about 1.5 miles up the lake's northeastern shore. Although the refuge is closed March 1 through July 1, floating on the river is still permitted in those months. *BOG ROAD IMPASSABLE IN SPRING; FOOT TRAVEL RECOMMENDED YEAR-ROUND.*

Directions: *Take Montana Highway 83 to the southern end of Swan Lake and look for the Swan River National Wildlife Refuge sign. A few hundred feet to the north of this sign is Bog Road.*

Ownership: USFWS (406) 755-7870
Size: 1,568 acres; 3- to 4-mile river float
Closest Town: Swan Lake

Great blue herons are stately birds of marshes, lakeshores, and streams. They are commonly seen along waterways in western Montana, including the Swan River.
RALEIGH MEADE

27

9. OLD SQUEEZER LOOP ROAD

Description: A small creek bottom at the foot of the Swan Mountain Range makes up this unique birding area. Both of the short loop trails (0.25 and 0.5 mile) have several benches for viewing and pass though grassy meadows, swamps, open hillsides, and timbered areas. Watch for Swainson's thrushes, redstarts, Vaux's swifts, hummingbirds, flycatchers, hairy woodpeckers, and warblers. May and June are usually the best months for birding. White-tailed deer and elk frequent the area. Black bear and mountain lion tracks can sometimes be found in soft or muddy areas along the trails. Look for white bog orchids in the wet areas along the road and trails.

Directions: *Follow Montana Highway 35 to the Swan River State Forest headquarters. Directly across from the headquarters, take Goat Creek Road (Forest Road 554) east for 1.5 miles. At the fork in the road, go right on Old Squeezer Loop Road and follow it for about 2 miles.*

Ownership: DSL (406) 542-4274
Size: 2-mile drive; 0.25- and 0.5-mile trails
Closest Town: Swan Lake

10. NINEPIPE NATIONAL WILDLIFE REFUGE, FWP AND TRIBAL WILDLIFE MANAGEMENT AREAS

Description: This exceptional wetland complex contains over 800 glacial potholes and a 1,770-acre reservoir. It's a terrific birding spot; about 200 bird species have been recorded here. A jointly managed viewing area is just off U.S. Highway 93 on the east side of the reservoir, about 0.75 mile south of the junction with Secondary Route 212. An access road and paved trail provide for waterfowl and shorebird viewing; the trail is barrier-free. Nesting great blue herons and double-crested cormorants can be observed from the dike road on west side of the refuge. Follow SR 212 along the north shore for 2 miles to the dike entrance to view ducks, grebes, and short-eared owls. Duck Road offers viewing of pothole ponds for about 2 miles; to reach it, turn west off U.S. 93, 1 mile north of SR 212. Superb viewing of raptors in winter. Area open to fall hunting.

Directions: *See map at right. From Ronan (45 miles north of Missoula), go south on U.S. Highway 93 for 4 miles and watch for refuge, Waterfowl Production Area, and Wildlife Management Area signs.*

Ownership: FWP, Confederated Salish-Kootenai Tribes, USFWS (406) 644-2211
Size: 9,000 acres   **Closest Town:** Ronan

11. NATIONAL BISON RANGE

Description: One of the oldest and most spectacular units in the entire national wildlife refuge system, this area contains steep, grassy hills and coniferous forests. It's a great example of the now rare, native Palouse prairie bunchgrass. The 300 to 500 bison are usually visible. In summer and early fall (mid-May through late October) visitors may drive either a scenic 2-hour loop (19 miles) or a shorter half-hour loop. The 1-hour winter drive and short loops are available for the balance of the year. Along the drive, you can view bison, pronghorn, elk, bighorn sheep, white-tailed and mule deer, and occasionally mountain goats, making the range ideal for wildlife photography. No off-road hiking is allowed except on designated trails. Seasonal highlights include newborn bison calves (mid-April through May), blue grouse mating rituals in forested areas (May), elk bugling (September), and bighorn sheep (summer). The area's 4 habitat types and 2,000-foot elevation change support more than 200 bird species. Look for Clark's nutcracker and Lewis' woodpecker in high forests, grasshopper sparrow in bunchgrasses, and lazuli bunting and yellow-breasted chat along Pauline Creek. The interpretive and education center has excellent wildlife exhibits. It is open daily in the summer, 8 a.m. - 8 p.m., and weekdays only in the winter, 8 a.m. - 4:30 p.m. *ENTRANCE FEE $4.00 PER VEHICLE; GOLDEN PASSES ACCEPTED.*

Directions: *From Missoula, take U.S. Highway 93 north to Ravalli. Drive west on Montana Highway 200 for 6 miles to Dixon, then north on Secondary Route 212 for 4 miles to the refuge entrance. Or, from Polson, take U.S. 93 to 4 miles south of Ronan. Turn right onto SR 212 and travel 13 miles to the entrance.*

Ownership: USFWS (406) 644-2211
Size: 18,541 acres   **Closest Town:** Moiese

Elk graze at the National Bison Range, one of western Montana's premier wildlife areas. Visitors are likely to see elk, bison, bighorn sheep, and pronghorn, along with smaller animals. MICHAEL S. SAMPLE

12. CLEARWATER CANOE TRAIL

Description: This truly exceptional 1- to 2-hour canoe trip flows through a dense willow marsh on an isolated portion of the Clearwater River. There's an information board with maps at the put-in. The float offers an outstanding opportunity to view warblers, nesting common loons, bitterns, catbirds, snipes, great blue herons, belted kingfishers, and common goldeneyes. Western painted turtles, large trout, muskrats, beavers, and dragonflies are common. It's a great place for kids and adults alike. The last part of the trip crosses the north end of Seeley Lake. A 30-minute (approximate) return hiking trail winds by the river and wetlands, eliminating shuttle problems and providing viewing access for non-floaters. On the trail, be sure to stop at the wildlife viewing blind, which allows great close-up views of waterfowl, yellow-headed blackbirds, sandhill cranes, and marsh-loving songbirds. Brochures about the canoe trail are available at the Seeley Lake Ranger Station.

Directions: *From Seeley Lake, drive 4 miles north on Montana Highway 83. Turn west at the Clearwater Canoe Trail sign and proceed 0.5 mile to the put-in. The canoe take-out and start of the return trail are at the Seeley Lake Ranger Station.*

Ownership: USFS (406) 677-2233
Size: 4-mile float, 1.5-mile return walk   **Closest Town:** Seeley Lake

13. SEELEY VALLEY CHAIN-OF-LAKES LOON DRIVING TOUR

Description: The Seeley Valley's highly scenic chain of lakes provides easy viewing of red-necked grebes, waterfowl, and osprey, as well as the largest population of nesting common loons in the western United States. Look for nests on the small islands or marshy sections of the lakes, but do not approach closer than 200 feet since the loons may abandon their nests. At the Salmon Lake wayside exhibit, view muskrat houses and bald eagles. At Alva Lake look for nesting osprey. At Seeley Lake, painted turtles and spotted frogs are common. White-tailed deer are abundant along the route. A tour brochure, "Loons of Seeley Lake," is available from the Forest Service at the Seeley Lake Ranger Station, just north of the town of Seeley Lake, and from the Lolo National Forest office in Missoula.

Directions: *From the junction of Montana Highway 83 and Montana Highway 200, drive north and stop at the designated points right off the road at Salmon, Seeley, and Alva Lakes.*

Ownership: USFS (406) 677-2233
Size: 18-mile drive   **Closest Town:** Seeley Lake

14. BLACKFOOT-CLEARWATER WILDLIFE MANAGEMENT AREA

Description: The rolling foothills and forests of this area contain considerable birdlife, including pileated woodpeckers, great gray owls, mountain bluebirds, and western tanagers. Along Cottonwood Creek, look for waterfowl, sandhill cranes, and bald eagles near some woodland ponds and wetlands. Tundra swans are sometimes spotted during migration. Wildlife checklists and a map are available at the FWP office in Missoula. The area is closed to all entry November 16 through May 15, yet large numbers of elk can be viewed from the Montana Highway 83 turnout during the winter months. Although there are no designated hiking trails, a number of roads can be driven or bicycled to view wildlife, and the gentle terrain lends itself to walking. Three miles northeast of the area, Upsata Lake is a predictable spot to see common loons and waterfowl. Area open to fall hunting.

Directions: *From Seeley Lake, take Montana Highway 83 south for 13 miles to the viewing area. Visitors can drive through the area by proceeding north on MT 83 to the first road going right (east). It's a fair dirt road, about 6 miles long and suitable for most cars. At the road's end, turn left and follow for 3 miles to Upsata Lake. A right turn takes drivers back to MT 200.*

Ownership: DSL, Plum Creek Timber Co., FWP (406) 542-5500
Size: 67,000 acres   **Closest Town:** Seeley Lake

15. KELLY ISLAND

Description: *URBAN SITE.* The habitat of this large, undeveloped island in the Clark Fork River is a unique mix of cottonwood bottoms, large meadows, and ponderosa pine forests with remarkable wildlife populations. Waterfowl concentrate here in the winter and spring; the numerous backwater sloughs provide ideal resting spots. Around March, great blue herons begin to gather.at the island's historic heron nesting area. Canada geese also nest on the island, sometimes in the heron nests. Wood duck boxes and goose nesting platforms have been erected here. Red-tailed hawks, American kestrels, and great horned owls commonly nest on the islands as well. This is a good spot to see Lewis' woodpecker and bald eagles. White-tailed deer are extremely abundant and seen year-round; beavers are common, and foxes are seen occasionally. River crossing can be difficult, but it's easy to get around on the island because of a myriad of well-worn animal trails. Visitors at other times can either boat or wade across the river. *DO NOT ATTEMPT TO WADE RIVER DURING SPRING OR OTHER PERIODS OF HIGH WATER.*

Directions: *In Missoula, take Spurgin Road west off Reserve Street to the fishing access site on the south side of Kelly Island, or take Mullan Road about 4 miles west off Reserve Street to the Kelly Island Fishing Access Site on the north side.*

Ownership: FWP (406) 542-5500
Size: 648 acres   **Closest Town:** Missoula

Widespread throughout Montana, the great horned owl may be seen in such diverse habitats as coniferous forests, bottom lands, even open plains, as long as cliffs or wooded areas are nearby. Great horned owls hunt rabbits, rodents, and such birds as ducks, crows, and other owls. TOM J. ULRICH

16. GREENOUGH PARK

Description: *URBAN SITE.* This outstanding city park runs along clean and beautiful Rattlesnake Creek for about 1 mile and is a diverse mix of cottonwood bottomlands and coniferous forest. A paved trail runs the length of the park and numerous unpaved paths go near the creek and toward more undisturbed places. A series of interpretive signs along the trails identify the most commonly seen birds; more than 100 bird species have been identified here. In the spring and summer it's an especially good area to see warblers, vireos, orioles, and black-headed grosbeaks. In the winter look for pygmy owls, pine grosbeaks, and hordes of Bohemian waxwings. Along the stream watch for American dippers, belted kingfishers, and spotted sandpipers. Pileated woodpeckers are also frequently sighted, and white-tailed deer and an occasional black bear (early mornings in the fall) can be seen.

Directions: *From Interstate 90 at Missoula, take the Van Buren Avenue exit and travel north on Van Buren Ave. Turn left (west) on Locust and go 2 blocks, then right (north) on Monroe, and look for the sign indicating Greenough Park.*

Ownership: City of Missoula (406) 721-7275
Size: 42 acres   **Closest Town:** Missoula

Just a short distance from downtown Missoula, Greenough Park is home to more than 100 bird species, including the pileated woodpecker.   MELISSA BLUNT

17. WILLOUGHBY ENVIRONMENTAL EDUCATION AREA AND CHARLES WATER NATURE TRAIL

Description: These 2 national forest areas in the beautiful Bitterroot Valley are part of a watchable wildlife viewing triangle that also includes the Lee Metcalf National Wildlife Refuge (site 18 in this book). At the Willoughby Environmental Education Area, sagebrush grassland communities are interspersed with ponderosa pine forests and a small creek. A 1-mile interpretive trail begins at the parking area. Look for red-tailed hawks spring through fall and rough-legged hawks in winter, soaring above the open shrub lands. Also common are western meadowlarks, mountain bluebirds, and savannah and vesper sparrows. Year-round residents include white-tailed deer, pine squirrels, great horned owls, and mountain and black-capped chickadees. The Charles Water Nature Trail is 18 miles northeast off U.S. Highway 93. The 0.5-mile trail traverses 2 dramatically different habitats that exist side by side. The trail begins in a dry ponderosa pine forest and quickly makes the transition to a cool, moist river bottom forest along Bass Creek. White-tailed deer are common, and elk, mule deer, and black bears are occasional visitors. Look for nuthatches, golden-crowned kinglets, dark-eyed juncos, and red crossbills year-round. Migratory bird species that are relatively common include ruby-crowned kinglets, warbling vireos, and western wood pewees.

Directions: *To reach Willoughby from Missoula, take U.S. Highway 93 south 35 miles. Turn east at Bell Crossing and follow Bell Crossing and Willoughby Lane (Bell Crossing turns into Willoughby) east 3 miles. Turn north onto South Sunset Bench Road and follow north and east 5 miles to the area. To reach the Charles Water Nature Trail, take U.S. 93 south 25 miles from Missoula and turn west on Bass Creek Road. Go west for 2 miles, and park at the parking area just after crossing Bass Creek. The trail starts 50 yards north of the parking area on Forest Road 1316. Interpretive trail guides for both areas are available from the Stevensville Ranger Station.*

Ownership: USFS (406) 777-5461
Size: 1.5 miles of trail   **Closest Town:** Stevensville

Eggs can chill quickly in Montana's weather, so be careful not to flush birds from their nests in spring. If you do so, move away to allow parents to return.

34

18. LEE METCALF NATIONAL WILDLIFE REFUGE

Description: Tiny by refuge standards (2,800 acres), this site has a diverse habitats and natural scenic beauty; it is a delightful environment for observing and photographing wildlife. Although managed primarily for migratory waterfowl, the refuge's wetlands, river bottom woodlands, and open fields are also home to white-tailed deer, coyotes, beavers, muskrats, otters, owls, woodpeckers, and a variety of songbirds. Wildfowl Lane, a county road, traverses the southern portion of the refuge where certain areas are open to the public for wildlife viewing. Visitors can observe nesting osprey and Canada geese, bald eagles, great blue herons, and a variety of waterfowl along this road, especially during peak migration periods in fall and early spring. A year-round day use area with picnicking and toilet facilities is located along Wildfowl Ln. Here, foot trails (including a 0.5-mile barrier-free trail to the picnic area) meander through 160 acres of open pine and cottonwood stands to the Bitterroot River. There is no drinking water and no indoor facilities on the refuge.

Directions: *Take U.S. Highway 93 to Stevensville, then turn east onto Montana Eastside Highway 203 and follow to Wildfowl Lane. Take this road for 1.5 miles until you see the refuge boundary signs. The refuge can also be reached from Florence off MT Eastside 203 to Wildfowl Lane.*

Ownership: USFWS (406) 777-5552
Size: 2,800 acres   **Closest Town:** Stevensville

At places such as the Lee Metcalf National Wildlife Refuge, nesting osprey are frequently seen. Watch from a distance to allow these birds to raise their young undisturbed. HARRY ENGELS

19. SKALKAHO WILDLIFE PRESERVE

Description: This isolated, mountainous wildlife preserve is forested with dense spruce and subalpine fir, amid beautiful lush meadows. The area is totally closed to hunting. In the spring and summer, look for gray and Steller's jays, dark-eyed juncos, Brewer's sparrows, olive-sided flycatchers, and hairy woodpeckers. Visitors in the fall may see large concentrations of elk and hear bull elk bugle from the high basins in early morning or late evening, especially east of Fool Hen and Kneaves Lakes. Hikers can see mountain goats around Dome Shaped Mountain, near the junction of trails 313 and 86, which follow the ridge around Skalkaho Basin. Watch for moose along trail 321 in the Burnt Fork drainage. Mule deer, badgers, coyotes, and black bears are common throughout the preserve. Mountain bicycling is a good way to see wildlife, especially during the fall road closure period, October 15 through December 1. Trail 313 offers prime opportunities for overnight cross-country ski trips. Since only the first 10 miles of Montana Highway 38 are plowed, winter viewing by car depends on snow depth.

Directions: *From Hamilton, travel 3 miles south on U.S. Highway 93, then turn east on Montana Highway 38 (Skalkaho Highway) and proceed 26 miles east to the top of the pass (20 miles is gravel). Turn north on Forest Road 1352 (closed to all motorized vehicles October 15 through December 1) and drive for 5 miles into the Skalkaho Basin (past Dam Lake). A wildlife interpretive sign and orientation map is on FR 1352 right after turning off MT 38.*

Ownership: USFS (406) 363-7161
Size: 23,000 acres   **Closest Town:** Hamilton

20. EAST FORK BIGHORN SHEEP HERD

Description: The rocky hillsides and grassy slopes above the East Fork of the Bitterroot River provide exceptional year-round bighorn sheep viewing. View the sheep from turnouts along the first 6 miles of the road and from the parking lot of the Broad Axe Lodge and Restaurant. Two wayside exhibits, one at Bunch Gulch (4 miles up the East Fork) and one near the Broad Axe (5.5 miles up), offer information as well as good vantage points for viewing. Golden eagles frequently soar over the hills, elk and white-tailed deer are common in the winter, and nighthawks are often seen in the summer dusk. Also in the summer, see large numbers of hummingbirds attracted by feeders surrounding the restaurant. The restaurant provides binoculars upon request so guests may view sheep while dining. Non-diners are welcome any time in the parking area.

Directions: *Take U.S. Highway 93 to Sula, then turn east on East Fork Road, which parallels the East Fork of the Bitterroot River, scanning for sheep along the first 6 miles. View from signed turnouts and the Broad Axe Lodge and Restaurant parking lot.*

Ownership: USFS (406) 821-3201,
Broad Axe Restaurant (406) 821-3878
Size: 3,200 acres   **Closest Town:** Sula

REGION TWO: GOLD WEST COUNTRY

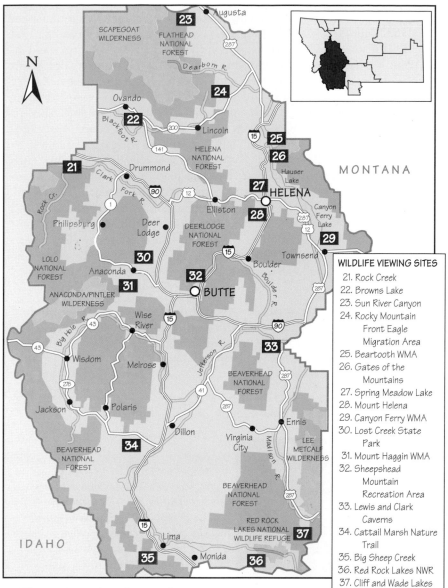

WILDLIFE VIEWING SITES

21. Rock Creek
22. Browns Lake
23. Sun River Canyon
24. Rocky Mountain Front Eagle Migration Area
25. Beartooth WMA
26. Gates of the Mountains
27. Spring Meadow Lake
28. Mount Helena
29. Canyon Ferry WMA
30. Lost Creek State Park
31. Mount Haggin WMA
32. Sheepshead Mountain Recreation Area
33. Lewis and Clark Caverns
34. Cattail Marsh Nature Trail
35. Big Sheep Creek
36. Red Rock Lakes NWR
37. Cliff and Wade Lakes

This region is best known for its towering mountains, broad valleys, and world-famous rivers and lakes. It's also rich in history, a place where ghost towns remain as reminders of mining's boom-and-bust era. The trumpeter swan was saved from near-extinction at Red Rock Lakes, one of the most picturesque national wildlife refuges in the nation. The sagebrush hills and forested uplands of the rugged Beartooth Wildlife Management Area support elk and prairie dogs. The rolling prairie abruptly meets the rugged peaks of the Rocky Mountains at spectacular Sun River Canyon, home to one of the largest herds of bighorn sheep in North America. At Lewis and Clark Caverns, western big-eared bats roost among the stalactites and other intriguing cave features.

21. ROCK CREEK

Description: Rock Creek is a nationally famous trout stream noted for its water quality and beautiful scenery. In June, the creek experiences an amazing insect hatch of giant stoneflies (known as salmon flies), which lay their eggs and attract trout. At the Valley of the Moon, the Rock Creek Nature Trail winds through cottonwood habitat teeming with wildlife. The 0.25-mile barrier-free trail crosses 2 footbridges and includes 10 trailside interpretive signs featuring the reasons why Rock Creek is such a great place for fish and wildlife. This is a good place to see trout, yellow warblers, cedar waxwings, red-naped sapsuckers, and beavers. The Babcock Mountain Bighorn Sheep Viewing Area (3 miles farther south along Rock Creek Road) has steep, grassy hillsides with rocky cliffs bordered by coniferous forest. It is an excellent place to see bighorn sheep, either from your car or while hiking. Hikers may walk the Babcock Creek Trail, which follows the face of the sheep range for about a mile. *TRAIL CLOSED DURING LAMBING SEASON, MID-APRIL THROUGH EARLY MAY.* The herd of about 150 animals is most visible in spring and winter, and may also be seen along Rock Creek Rd. south of Babcock Creek for about 6 miles. During spring lambing season, ewes and lambs can usually be seen on the rocky cliffs. The bitterroot, Montana's state flower, blooms in June on hot, dry sites.

Directions: From Missoula, drive 20 miles east on Interstate 90, exiting at Rock Creek. Travel south on Rock Creek Road for 2 miles, turning right at the Valley of the Moon to reach the Rock Creek Nature Trail. Babcock Mountain Bighorn Sheep Viewing Area is 5 miles south of I-90 along Rock Creek Rd. Watch for an informational sign.

Ownership: PVT, USFS (406) 329-3814
Size: 8,000 acres   **Closest Town:** Clinton

The giant stonefly, which survives only in rivers and streams with high water quality, lives for three years in its nymphal stage, hidden beneath rocks on the streambed. When spring water temperatures reach 50 degrees or more, the stonefly crawls ashore to shed its nymphal husk and dry its three-inch-long wings.
DALE C. SPARTAS

22. BROWNS LAKE AND BLACKFOOT WATERFOWL PRODUCTION AREA

Description: Browns Lake is a shallow, productive 500-acre lake surrounded by open sagebrush grasslands and aspen groves. It's an extremely reliable place to see both bald eagles and osprey (especially in the spring), and almost always has significant numbers of waterfowl. The marsh in the lake's northeast corner is a good place to see American coots, grebes, and great blue herons and a likely spot for American avocets, yellow-headed blackbirds, and broods of Canada geese. Sandhill cranes, common loons, American white pelicans, and upland sandpipers are often seen here in the spring. Black terns, uncommon in this area, nest on Browns Lake. Most birds are easily observed from a fair dirt road that goes halfway around the lake. Mountain bicycling and canoeing are good ways to see this area; please note, however, that the northeast corner of the lake is closed to boating during the nesting season (April 1 through July 15). The 1,539-acre Blackfoot Waterfowl Production Area (WPA) lies adjacent to Browns Lake on the east. Numerous seasonal and semi-permanent wetlands attract a wide variety of nesting shorebirds and waterfowl. Sandhill cranes nest on the WPA. Riparian areas along the Blackfoot River attract numerous songbirds. A summer climb up Marcum Mountain, just north of Montana Highway 200, gives an interpretive overlook and may reward a determined hiker with a glimpse of a blue grouse brood. During the winter, large numbers of elk and deer can often be seen from the highway. *BLACKFOOT WPA OPEN TO FOOT TRAVEL ONLY. DOGS PROHIBITED IN WPA APRIL 1 THROUGH AUGUST 30.*

Directions: *Take Montana Highway 200 to Ovando, then follow the fishing access signs to Browns Lake. To reach the WPA interpretive display, follow the Browns Lake road around the lake and continue east until you circle back to MT 200. The display on MT 200 is a short distance from this junction.*

Ownership: PVT, USFWS, FWP (406) 542-5500
Size: 2,000 acres   **Closest Town:** Ovando

Forest fires are good news for the black-backed woodpecker, which seeks out trees recently killed by fire, searching for insects under the blackened bark.

The Sun River area contains one of the largest native herds of bighorn sheep in North America.   MICHAEL S. SAMPLE

23. SUN RIVER CANYON

Description: At Sun River Canyon, the rolling prairies of the Northern Great Plains abruptly meet the rugged peaks of the Rockies, with steep cliffs and dramatic terrain. The area has exceptional wildlife diversity and abundance, with one of the largest herds of bighorn sheep in North America (800 to 1,000 animals). To view sheep, stop at the bighorn sheep viewing and interpretive area, approximately 2 miles west after crossing the national forest boundary on the Sun Canyon Road. Sun River Canyon is also a good area to see elk, deer, and raptors—especially eagles, which migrate in significant numbers along the edge of the mountains. Mountain lions use this area extensively; look for their tracks following a snowfall. In the summer, look for beavers and songbirds along the slough near the river. In the winter and spring, the bighorn sheep are especially visible close to the road, which is well maintained and plowed. Immediately southeast of Sun River Canyon is the State of Montana's 20,000-acre Sun River Wildlife Management Area (WMA), which winters one of the state's largest elk populations. The WMA is closed to public access in winter, but elk can be viewed from any of several nearby roads. In summer, drive, hike, or mountain bicycle in the WMA to see Canada geese and great blue herons on numerous small lakes; visitors may also see sharp-tailed grouse, coyotes, grizzly and black bears, bighorn sheep, wolves and long-billed curlews on the grassy uplands. The WMA is open to fall hunting. This area along the Rocky Mountain Front is the heart of the chinook belt, providing some the earliest wildflower displays (April) east of the Rockies.

Directions: *At Augusta, turn northwest off of U.S. Highway 287 onto the Sun River Road. Follow this road for 4 miles, turning right at the fork in the road. Proceed northwest for about 15 miles to Sun River Canyon.*

Ownership: FWP, USFS (406) 562-3247
Size: 4,000 acres   **Closest Town:** Augusta

Look for signs of bear activity on trees. Bears often rip apart the outer bark of a tree to feed on the sweet, inner bark, leaving a triangular scar on the trunk.

24. ROCKY MOUNTAIN FRONT EAGLE MIGRATION AREA

Description: This scenic mountain area is part of a major spring migration route for eagles (primarily golden, but some bald) along the east front of the Rocky Mountains, where in March the strong westerly winds rushing over the foothills create the lift eagles need for high flight. In fact, this area is where the most eagles have been observed in North America in a single day. During key migration times, eagles can sometimes be seen in large numbers from a distance of 100 to 500 feet. The best springtime eagle-watching is in March (as many as 818 golden eagles and 129 bald eagles have been seen between March 12 and April 3), but migration continues through May. A viewing site on the east side of Rogers Pass features a wayside interpretive exhibit. Migration usually begins 9 a.m. - 10 a.m. and peaks 3 p.m. - 5 p.m. Other raptors to look for are red-tailed hawks, rough-legged hawks, sharp-shinned hawks, and northern goshawks. *LAND ADJACENT TO VIEWING SITE IS PRIVATE PROPERTY; PLEASE RE-SPECT THE RIGHTS OF PRIVATE LANDOWNERS.*

Directions: *From Lincoln, drive east on Montana Highway 200 for 27 miles to the viewing site, about 9 miles beyond Rogers Pass. Watch for the binocular signs.*

Ownership: USFS (406) 362-4265
Size: **Closest Town:** Lincoln

25. BEARTOOTH WILDLIFE MANAGEMENT AREA

Description: The beautiful grass and sagebrush hills of this Wildlife Management Area (WMA) gradually give way to forested uplands with rugged rocky outcroppings. The site is notable for its large populations of elk and bighorn sheep. The WMA is easily accessible via good dirt roads, where wildlife can be viewed from the car. Hikers can walk up one of the roads that follows a creek (Cottonwood, Elkhorn, and Willow Creeks are good bets), some of which are closed to vehicle use (Cottonwood year-round, and Elkhorn September 1 through November 30) but open to mountain bicycling. Go up one of the creek bottoms, then follow one of the ridgelines back down. Birding is especially good along Cottonwood Creek downstream to the lake, and ridge hikes often lead to sighting of bighorn sheep, deer, and elk. Look for a prairie dog town on the north side of the road not far past the boundary of the WMA; there's an informational sign. This WMA is open to fall hunting. *AREA CLOSED TO PUBLIC USE DECEMBER 1 THROUGH MAY 14.*

Directions: *From Helena, take Interstate 15 north to Wolf Creek. Turn north on the Missouri River Road until you reach the Holter Lake access road. Follow this road along the east shore of Holter Lake for about 6 miles to the Beartooth WMA.*

Ownership: FWP (406) 454-3441
Size: 31,798 acres   **Closest Town:** Wolf Creek

26. GATES OF THE MOUNTAINS

Description: The Missouri River from Canyon Ferry Dam to Holter Dam ranges from only a few hundred feet wide to over a mile across, and passes through mountains, foothills, valleys, canyons, and prairie lands. The Gates of the Mountains section is one of the most scenic along the Missouri River corridor. The best way to see this area is by boat. Boat trips along this spectacular section of the Missouri often provide close-up views of bighorn sheep, mountain goats, and mule deer. Along the length of the corridor look for bald eagles, osprey, red-tailed hawks, turkey vultures, great horned owls, river otters, peregrine falcons, and American white pelicans. There are numerous trails along the corridor that offer additional wildlife viewing opportunities (3 trails lead from the Meriwether Picnic Area, and 1 trail runs along the river from Hauser Dam to Beaver Creek Road). Tour boats leave from Upper Holter Lake and go north through the Gates of the Mountains.

Directions: *From Helena, drive 20 miles north on Interstate 15 and take the Gates of the Mountains exit, Exit 209. Proceed 2.8 miles to Upper Holter Lake. There is a public boat launch here, in addition to the private boat tours. There are also numerous fishing access sites with boat launches along the entire Missouri River corridor.*

Ownership: Montana Power Co., BLM, USFS, FWP (406) 444-1276, PVT boat tours (406) 458-5241
Size: 38-mile stretch of river
Closest Town: Helena

27. SPRING MEADOW LAKE

Description: *URBAN SITE.* The centerpiece of this small park is a crystalline, spring-fed lake surrounded by willows and cottonwoods. Nearby uplands with sagebrush and rabbitbrush add to the diverse habitat. Spring Meadow Lake is a solid birding spot during migration times and often has Canada geese, American coots, mallards, and occasionally common loons. The willows and cottonwoods harbor warblers, vireos, and other songbirds. This dense lakeside vegetation also houses rabbits, muskrats, and skunks. On summer evenings visitors can usually see bats or nighthawks. Five kinds of non-poisonous snakes have been reported in the area, and the clear waters are alive with painted turtles, trout, largemouth bass, and perch. Heavy swimming use at the north end of the lake can reduce wildlife viewing opportunities in the summer. But early in the morning, or at other times of year, it affords good wildlife watching very close to town. There's a 1-mile nature trail around the lake with wildlife information signs; brochures are available at the park entrance.

Directions: *In Helena, follow U.S. Highway 12 west toward Missoula. Before you leave town, turn right (north) on Joslyn Street, then curve left onto Country Club Avenue and follow the sign to Spring Meadow Lake.*

Ownership: FWP (406) 444-3750
Size: 56 acres; 1-mile trail
Closest Town: Helena

28. MOUNT HELENA

Description: *URBAN SITE.* Mount Helena is a large, wild city park that adjoins nearly 11,000 acres of undeveloped national forest land. A variety of wildlife inhabits its scattered Douglas-fir forests and expansive grassland areas. Two well-marked trails leave the parking area and circle the mountain, climbing 1,200 feet to Mount Helena's mile-high summit. For the best wildlife viewing on a short walk, follow trail #1906 as it leaves the parking area to the west. After about 200 yards turn right on the Prairie Trail at the first marked trail junction. Prairie Trail gently climbs for 2 miles through open grasslands below the towering limestone cliffs near the intersection with the Westside Trail. The expansive view along the edge of the cliffs and forests provides opportunities to see yellow-rumped warblers, western tanagers, mountain bluebirds, western meadowlarks, rufous-sided and green-tailed towhees, red-breasted nuthatches, juncos, ravens, and vesper sparrows. Follow the Westside Trail to the Mount Helena Ridge National Recreation Trail for 7 more miles of open ridge walking.

Directions: *In downtown Helena, take Park Avenue south to Clarke Street. Turn right on Clarke, and left on Benton Avenue. From Benton, take Adams Street west (right) to parking area and kiosk describing regulations and trails.*

Ownership: City of Helena (406) 447-8463
Size: 620 acres   **Closest Town:** Helena

29. CANYON FERRY WMA AND RESERVOIR

Description: An exceptional wetland and river bottom area, this site where the Missouri River enters Canyon Ferry Reservoir is a good place to see migrating waterfowl and many nesting birds: Canada geese, double-crested cormorants, American white pelicans, Caspian terns, and osprey. Commonly seen mammals include white-tailed deer and beavers; river otters and moose are seen infrequently. The best place to see mammals is in the delta portion of the Wildlife Management Area (WMA). This area can be reached via numerous gravel roads off the east side of U.S. Highway 287. The best place to view waterfowl and shorebirds is Pond 3 on the east side of the WMA. A map of the WMA is available from the USFS and FWP offices in Townsend. WMA open to fall hunting. *NEARBY VIEWING OPPORTUNITY:* between mid-October and mid-December a large number of bald eagles—as many as 300—typically congregate at the opposite end of Canyon Ferry Reservoir below Canyon Ferry Dam to feed on spawning kokanee salmon. More than 1,000 bald eagles pass through during migration, one of the largest congregations in the lower 48 states.

Directions: *The WMA begins 1 mile north of Townsend and continues for 2 miles along the east side of U.S. Highway 287. It can be reached by several gravel roads that turn off U.S. 287. Or, from Townsend, follow U.S. Highway 12 east for a short distance, then turn north onto Harrison Road. To view eagles at the reservoir, turn east onto Secondary Route 284 off U.S. 12 about 9 miles east of Helena, and proceed 12 miles to the dam's visitor center. Follow signs to the eagle viewing area.*

Ownership: BOR, WMA managed by FWP (406) 475-3310
Size: 5,000 acres   **Closest Town:** Townsend

30. LOST CREEK STATE PARK

Description: Lost Creek is a small state park in a narrow canyon with 1,200+ foot high limestone cliffs and a small stream with a beautiful falls. The rocky cliffs provide a home for bighorn sheep as well as easily observable mountain goats. One of the best places to see the goats is from a pullout (marked with informational signs) at the park entrance. The best time to see the sheep is during winter and spring in the dry, open grasslands and scattered timber near the park entrance. Although the sheep aren't usually as visible during summer and fall, they can often be seen in the Olsen Gulch area (about 4 miles to the west). Moose are seen frequently in the creek bottom year-round, and mule deer often are sighted on the rocky hillsides. Look for black bears on the open hillsides in the spring. A short walk to Lost Creek Falls is the only established hiking trail. For a longer walk, follow the old road near the end of the park road; it goes west for about 6 miles before connecting to Foster Creek. Look for moose in the creek bottom and mule deer on the hillsides. The 2-mile park road is excellent for cross-country skiing and viewing winter wildlife. *PARK OPEN MAY 1 THROUGH NOVEMBER 30; FOOT TRAVEL ALLOWED YEAR-ROUND.*

Directions: *From Interstate 90, take Montana Highway 1 to Anaconda. Approximately 2 miles east of Anaconda take Galen Road, following signs to the park.*

Ownership: USFS, FWP (406) 542-5500
Size: 500 acres **Closest Town:** Anaconda

A pair of Canada geese lead their goslings on a quiet stretch of water. Canada geese nest along many rivers and lakes in Montana, including the Missouri River and Canyon Ferry Reservoir. MICHAEL S. SAMPLE

31. MOUNT HAGGIN WILDLIFE MANAGEMENT AREA

Description: Montana's second largest Wildlife Management Area, Mount Haggin is a stunning mix of aspen-dotted rolling hills, lush willow bottoms, and forested mountains, with the Pintler Range looming in the background. It's a great place to see moose, elk, and nesting sandhill cranes. Exceptional habitat diversity makes for good birding—look for warblers, vireos, and thrushes in the bottomlands and raptors and grouse in the uplands. Good viewing spots include Dry Creek Road (Forest Road 2483), about 1 mile north of the vista area, and Home Ranch Road, about 4 miles south of the vista area. Home Ranch Rd. is frequently impassable, so hiking or mountain bicycling is recommended. Another good viewing area is a large meadow only 0.5 mile up the road from the turnoff to Home Ranch. There are no established hiking trails, but there are many unmarked trails. Hikers are allowed to walk anywhere, and mountain bicyclists will find outstanding potential here. This area is open to fall hunting. A portion of Mount Haggin is open to cross-country skiing, when moose are particularly visible.

Directions: *From Anaconda, take Montana Highway 1 east for 3 miles until you reach Secondary Route 274. Heading south toward Wisdom, SR 274 bisects the WMA near the Continental Divide. Look for Mule Ranch Vista area about 14 miles from MT 1. There are informational signs on the west side of the road.*

Ownership: FWP (406) 994-4042
Size: 54,137 acres   **Closest Town:** Anaconda

32. SHEEPSHEAD MOUNTAIN RECREATION AREA

Description: This area is a mixture of meadows and marshes surrounded by lodgepole pine forests, streams, and a small lake. The day use area, trails, bathrooms, and even a fishing dock on Maney Lake are barrier-free. A 0.5-mile, paved interpretive trail (with a taprail and textured trail surface) beginning at the Freedom Point picnic pavilion has signs and audio recordings that talk about forest and water habitats and wildlife. It's a good place to see deer and occasionally a moose or elk. Waterfowl use the lake, especially during migration, and the paths along the small creek are usually alive with birds. Spotted sandpipers, killdeers, mountain bluebirds, nuthatches, and hairy and downy woodpeckers are commonly seen. The area is also home to pine squirrels, chipmunks, rabbits, badgers, and porcupines. The facility is open late May through September. Just south of Sheepshead on Forest Road 9485, the 16-mile long Hail Columbia Gulch Road from Sheepshead to Rocker is a fair gravel road that's good for wildlife viewing. Near the Lowland Campground, look for moose. Raptors are frequently seen in the meadows. Near the junction of Hail Columbia Gulch Rd. and the main road, look for warblers, vireos, and other birds in the thick streamside vegetation.

Directions: *From Butte, drive north on Interstate 15, exiting at Elk Park (mile post 138). Proceed west on Forest Road 442 for 6 miles, following signs to viewing area.*

Ownership: USFS (406) 494-2147
Size: 156 acres   **Closest Town:** Butte

33. LEWIS AND CLARK CAVERNS

Description: The beautiful limestone caverns of this state park are home to the only known maternity colony of western big-eared bats in Montana. Guided tours through the caverns take about 2 hours and are offered May 1 through September 30. The tour guide usually points out the bats. Hikers going through the caverns should also look for bushy-tailed wood rats. A self-guided nature trail to the cavern entrance explains the natural surroundings and is a good place to see birds, including rock and house wrens, mountain bluebirds, white-throated swifts, wild turkey, rufous hummingbirds, and both green-tailed and rufous-sided towhees. Prairie rattlesnakes, bull snakes, and racers can be found near the caverns and along the trail. On the drive to the caverns, look for raptors (especially golden eagles and red-tailed hawks) overhead along the Jefferson River. Mule deer and coyotes are common on the scenic 3-mile drive to the visitor center. Birdlists at Park Information Center and visitor center. Rustic cabins and a campground are open year-round. Contact FWP to rent cabins.

Directions: *From Three Forks, drive 19 miles west on Montana Highway 2.*

Ownership: FWP (406) 287-3541
Size: 3,000 acres   **Closest Town:** Three Forks

Montana's Lewis and Clark Caverns is one of the best places to view western big-eared bats. These animals require undisturbed roosting areas within the caverns. KRISTI DUBOIS

34. CATTAIL MARSH NATURE TRAIL

Description: Walking through this small, easily-accessible cattail marsh surrounded by dry uplands at the north end of Clark Canyon Reservoir is a good way to see birdlife. The marsh is very near the interstate, yet offers wildlife information signs and close-up views of waterfowl, blackbirds (yellow-headed as well as red-wing), rails, American coots, and common snipe. Look for cliff swallows and their mud nests on the rocky cliffs. Yellow-bellied marmots sun themselves on the rocks, while pronghorn range on the dry uplands. Trout can be viewed near the large spring on the west side of the trail. There's also great shorebird and waterfowl viewing about 5 miles from the cattail marsh area at the extensive mudflats near the south end of Clark Canyon Reservoir. Take the Red Rock exit off Interstate 15 and head north about 2.5 miles to a cattle guard. Cross the cattle guard and continue north toward the reservoir shore rather than following the main gravel road that turns west.

Directions: *From Dillon, drive south on Interstate 15 and take Exit 44 at Clark Canyon (Secondary Route 324). Follow the road over the dam and take the first right at the river fishing access sign. The barrier-free trail is an old paved road immediately below the dam, adjacent to the no-fee campground.*

Ownership: BOR (406) 683-6472
Size: 30 acres   **Closest Town:** Dillon

35. BIG SHEEP CREEK

Description: This isolated, spectacular mountain valley is a narrow canyon with a good dirt road that provides opportunities to view golden eagles, sandhill cranes, mule deer, pronghorn, and sometimes elk. A profusion of wildflowers blooms in early summer. Bighorn sheep, once prolific here, were hit by disease in the early 1990s; a few might still be spotted 4.5 miles up the road where the canyon gets narrow and rocky. Hikers might try the Hidden Pasture Trail (about 4 miles up the road), which heads south from Big Sheep Creek Road through open country with great views. Look for Townsend's solitaire, various warblers, red-tailed hawks, sharp-shinned hawks, and great horned owls. On Muddy Creek Road (about 6 miles from the frontage road), look for elk, deer, and mountain cottontails. This is also a reliable place to see pygmy rabbits, found only in the southwestern corner of Montana. There's a significant sage grouse population in the upper Big Sheep Creek area. One of the larger strutting grounds is about 20 miles from the frontage road, where Alkali Creek crosses the road in Section 2. The best viewing is during mid- to late April at morning's first light.

Directions: *Take Interstate 15 to the Dell exit, about 40 miles south of Dillon, then proceed south on the frontage road for 1.5 miles. Turn right onto Big Sheep Creek Road and follow it for about 4.5 miles.*

Ownership: BLM (406) 683-2337
Size: 12,000+ acres   **Closest Town:** Lima

36. RED ROCK LAKES NATIONAL WILDLIFE REFUGE

Description: Comprising nearly 13,000 acres of wetlands and peaks that rise sharply to over 9,000 feet, this large and extremely remote refuge has been called the most beautiful national wildlife refuge in the United States. The trumpeter swan was brought back from near-extinction here; 100 to 300 swans live and breed on the refuge, the largest breeding population in the lower 48 states. View swans from the Upper Lake Campground and the Lower Lake turnout; Shambow Pond and Wigeon Pond are also good. More than 50,000 ducks and geese may be present during fall migration. Shorebirds such as long-billed curlews, willets, and American avocets frequent the mudflats near the marshes, while gulls, terns, and American white pelicans are often viewed winging over the water. Look for songbirds, butterflies, and wildflowers at the Upper Lake Campground, as well as moose in the willows anywhere along the south shore of Upper Lake. Look for sandhill cranes west of Lower Red Rock Lake and in the uplands south of Upper Red Rock Lake. The Centennial Valley has a notable concentration of raptors, especially red-tailed, ferruginous and Swainson's hawks, and peregrine falcons. An exceptional day-long canoe trip between the upper and lower lakes (check with refuge headquarters for water levels and directions) is open from September 15 until freeze-up. There's good hiking along Odell or Red Rock Creeks, and bicycling on numerous unimproved roads. Check in at refuge headquarters at Lakeview for additional information.

Directions: *From Lima, follow Interstate 15 south to the Monida exit, then turn east on a gravel road and travel 28 miles on a good gravel road to the refuge entrance. From West Yellowstone, follow U.S. 20 to the junction with Montana 87. Proceed north on MT 87 for 5 miles and turn west onto Red Rock Pass Road, following a good gravel road for about 20 miles.*

Ownership: USFWS (406) 276-3536
Size: 45,117 acres   **Closest Town:** Lima

The Centennial Mountains on the Montana-Idaho border tower above Red Rocks Lakes National Wildlife Refuge. MICHAEL S. SAMPLE

37. CLIFF AND WADE LAKES

Description: Cliff and Wade Lakes sit on a geologic fault that formed a chasm that filled with water; cliffs surround much of the lakes' shorelines. Cliff Lake is the larger and somewhat more isolated of the two. Wade Lake is more easily accessible and receives more use; it's spring-fed and stays partly ice-free in the winter. Both lakes support many nesting raptors. Look for prairie falcons, bald eagles, and osprey—*DO NOT APPROACH OR DISTURB NESTING BIRDS.* Waterfowl and beavers are common on both lakes. In the winter, Wade Lake is a good place to see river otters and occasionally trumpeter swans. Larger mammals frequently seen include deer, elk, and moose, which are even more numerous and visible in the winter. Cliff Lake offers some exceptional canoeing, especially in the remote coves; canoes and lodging available at Wade Lake Resort (406) 682-7560. Hikers can learn something of the flora, fauna, and geology of the area on an 0.7-mile interpretive trail connecting the Wade Lake and Hilltop campgrounds. A newly developed spawning channel is an excellent place to view rainbow trout. The lakes also can be a great place for cross-country skiing in the winter.

Directions: *Just north of the junction of U.S. Highway 287 and Montana Highway 87, take Forest Road 8381. Follow this fair gravel road for about 6 miles to the lakes (look for signs).*

Ownership: USFS (406) 682-4253
Size: 890 acres
Closest Town: Ennis

Moose dwell in the wetter areas of western Montana, browsing on willows and aquatic plants in summer. Always view moose from a safe distance.   MICHAEL S. SAMPLE

REGION THREE:
CHARLIE RUSSELL COUNTRY

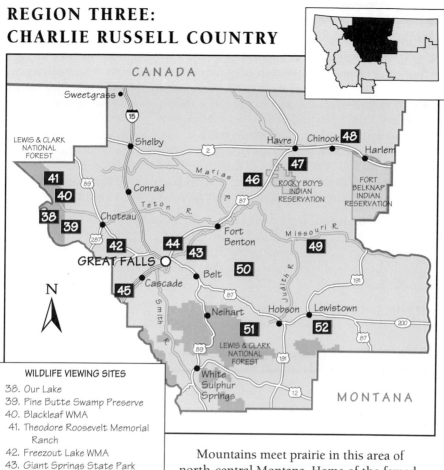

WILDLIFE VIEWING SITES

38. Our Lake
39. Pine Butte Swamp Preserve
40. Blackleaf WMA
41. Theodore Roosevelt Memorial Ranch
42. Freezout Lake WMA
43. Giant Springs State Park
44. Benton Lake NWR
45. Missouri River Recreation Road
46. Lonesome Lake
47. Beaver Creek County Park
48. BR-12 Prairie Marsh
49. Missouri Wild and Scenic River
50. Square Butte
51. Judith River WMA
52. Big Springs Trout Hatchery

Mountains meet prairie in this area of north-central Montana. Home of the famed western artist Charlie Russell, this land still looks like the cowboy country he depicted in the 1800s: big sky, expansive prairie grasslands, buttes, and wetlands. One of its most notable features is the Missouri River, which flows for more than 200 miles. A 149-mile segment of the river is part of the National Wild and Scenic Rivers system. It offers an abundance of wildlife, including a prairie elk herd and more than 200 species of songbirds. Freezout Lake Wildlife Management Area is a vast wetland complex that typically attracts the highest concentrations of shorebirds and migratory waterfowl found in the state. Pine Butte Swamp Preserve, managed by The Nature Conservancy, features wetlands and prairie grasslands that support grizzly bears, sharp-tailed grouse, and an abundance of coyotes.

38. OUR LAKE

Description: One of the few alpine lakes along the Rocky Mountain Front, Our Lake is a dependable place to see mountain goats. On the 3.5-mile hike to the lake look for bluebirds and three-toed woodpeckers in a burn area. Mountain goats can usually be spotted near the lake or on the nearby cliffs and have adapted to people—please keep your distance from goats; do not feed them or any other wildlife. Pikas and yellow-bellied marmots inhabit the rocky scree. Yellowstone cutthroat trout are often visible in the clear lake. Grizzly bears, mule deer, coyotes, grouse, pine marten, and eagles are area residents. Wildflowers are abundant. The lake is used heavily on weekends. It's normally accessible June through October, but July and August are the only sure access times, due to weather. *CAMPING PROHIBITED WITHIN 1,000 FEET OF LAKESHORE.*

Directions: *From Choteau, drive north on U.S. Highway 89 for 5 miles. Turn west on County Road 144 (Teton Road) and follow it for 15 miles. At the Ear Mountain Ranger Station sign, turn south on County Road 109 (South Fork Teton Road) and drive 9 miles to the end of the road. Hike along Forest Service trail #184 for 3.5 miles to Our Lake.*

Ownership: USFS (406) 466-5341
Size: 700 acres; 3.5-mile trail   **Closest Town:** Choteau

39. PINE BUTTE SWAMP PRESERVE

Description: Pine Butte, a unique private preserve, is the largest wetland complex along the Rocky Mountain Front and one of the grizzly bear's last strongholds on the plains. A sandstone butte looms 500 feet above the prairie, encircled on the north and west by a dense swamp called a *fen*. This swamp provides important habitat for the grizzly bear (the chances of actually seeing a bear are remote) and more than 43 other mammals including beavers, muskrats, deer, and elk. Watch coyotes stalk their prey on the rolling grasslands. More than 150 bird species have been recorded here, from warblers and vireos to long-billed curlews, sandhill cranes, and upland sandpipers. LeConte's sparrow is a species of special concern. Sharp-tailed grouse are common, especially on several dancing grounds in the spring. The A. B. Guthrie Trail across the road from the information kiosk offers a good view of the butte and surrounding swamp. Access to the rest of the preserve is limited to protect natural features. Contact the preserve manager, (406) 466-5526, for permission to walk in the swamp or on the butte. Weekly stays with guided tours are available May through September at the Pine Butte Guest Ranch, (406) 466-2158.

Directions: *From Choteau, drive north on U.S. Highway 89 for 5 miles. Turn west on Teton Canyon Road and follow for 17 miles. Turn south, cross the Teton River, and proceed straight for 3.5 miles following signs to an information kiosk.*

Ownership: The Nature Conservancy (406) 466-5526
Size: 18,000 acres   **Closest Town:** Choteau

40. BLACKLEAF WILDLIFE MANAGEMENT AREA

Description: Limber pine on glacial outwash areas, rolling grasslands, and marshes form splendid winter range for elk and deer on the flanks of the Rocky Mountain Front. Outstanding wildflower displays can be seen in spring and early summer. Probably the best place to view wildlife is Antelope Butte, a sandstone escarpment that escaped the glaciers. Grizzly and black bears frequent the area (parts of the WMA are closed each spring until July 1 due to grizzly use), as do mule deer and elk. At the south end of the butte are marshes and ponds with willows and aspen—good places to walk and look for waterfowl, shorebirds, and numerous songbirds. A variety of raptors can be seen in the area: marsh hawks, Swainson's hawks, red-tailed hawks, golden eagles, merlins, and prairie falcons. Marmots and ground squirrels provide a solid prey base for raptors and coyotes. Look for sharp-tailed grouse dancing in the spring. The best time to see elk is in winter.*OFF-ROAD TRAVEL PROHIBITED DECEMBER 1 THROUGH MAY 15 TO PROTECT WINTERING ANIMALS.* The county road is plowed to the east end of the WMA. A herd of about 75 mountain goats can be seen year-round where the road dead-ends in stunningly beautiful Blackleaf Canyon. Park and walk west for less than a mile to where the canyon narrows. On the hike in, look for whitewashed areas on the canyon walls to spot nesting raptors. WMA open to fall hunting.

Directions: *Take U.S. Highway 89 to Bynum, and then drive west on Blackleaf Road for about 16 miles to the WMA. Dirt Roads to WMA are not well marked. Oil and gas drilling take place on WMA.*

Ownership: FWP (406) 454-3441
Size: 19,430 acres   **Closest Town:** Bynum

Sharp-tailed grouse perform elaborate mating displays on historic breeding grounds known as "leks," to which they return each year. These fascinating spring rituals may be observed from a distance at Pine Butte Swamp Preserve and Blackleaf Wildlife Management Area, among other places. MICHAEL S. SAMPLE

41. THEODORE ROOSEVELT MEMORIAL RANCH

Description: This private ranch encompasses wet meadows and cottonwood river bottoms, rolling hills of shortgrass prairie, limber pine, and Douglas-fir and aspen stands covering the slopes and great limestone reefs of the spectacular Rocky Mountain Front. A kiosk and 0.5-mile trail are in the planning stages; these will overlook the ranch. In the bottomlands look for a variety of birds, including Cassin's finches, mountain bluebirds, western meadowlarks, northern flickers, and pileated woodpeckers. Look for white-tailed deer in the bottoms, too. The plains and hillsides are home to ruffed, blue, and sharp-tailed grouse, and as many as 2,000 mule deer and 600 elk in the winter. Red-tailed hawks nest on the ranch and can be heard and seen daily spring through fall near Dupuyer Creek. Beavers are common in Dupuyer Creek and its feeder streams. Although quite secretive and rarely seen, wolves, grizzly bears, black bears, bobcats, and mountain lions also appear on the ranch. With the exception of the trail and kiosk area, the ranch is closed to public access except by written permission from ranch headquarters. Foot and horseback access on the road is open year-round, but vehicle access is limited to May 15 through October 15. The road (often referred to as Dupuyer Creek Road) provides access to adjacent national forest land; much of the ranch and its wildlife can be viewed from this road. *NO FACILITIES. ACCESS TO KIOSK AND NATURE TRAIL CLOSED DURING FALL HUNTING SEASON, MID-OCTOBER THROUGH DECEMBER 1.*

Directions: *See map at right. From U.S. Highway 89 at Dupuyer, take Dupuyer Creek Road west for 8.5 miles. Take the left fork in the road and go south 0.5 mile to a T; go left on county road about 3 miles to another T; go right about 2 miles to top of hill past cattle guard. The kiosk is at the top of the hill*

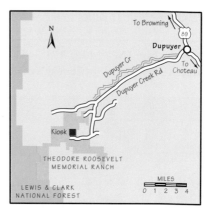

Ownership: Boone and Crockett Club (406) 472-3380
Size: 6,040 acres
Closest Town: Dupuyer

 About one-fourth of the birds in Montana's forests are cavity nesters. These birds depend on standing dead trees for their nesting sites. They may also make homes within the heartwood of living trees.

Description: Up to a million birds stop at Freezout Lake when migration peaks in spring and fall (March through May, September through November). As many as 300,000 snow geese and 10,000 tundra swans have been observed at one time here. The third week in March and the first week in November are peak dates for tundra swan migrations; the first week in April and the first week in November are peak times for snow geese. In spring, migration numbers are usually larger. Freezout Lake is also noted for its upland birds and shorebirds. Birds of special interest include American egrets, white-faced ibis, black-crowned night herons, sandhill cranes, and black-necked stilts. Thousands of California, ring-billed, and Franklin's gulls have been banded at the refuge, with returns from as far away as Peru. During winter the most visible bird species include ring-necked pheasants, sharp-tailed grouse, gray partridges, bald and golden eagles, rough-legged hawks, rare gyrfalcons, great horned owls, and an occasional snowy owl. Coyotes, foxes, jackrabbits, and long-tailed weasels also may be seen. This WMA has very good access—the only closures are during the waterfowl hunting season (October through December) to provide a resting area for waterfowl. Hiking and canoeing are possible anywhere outside the closure. The headquarters office immediately off U.S. Highway 89 has maps delineating the closed area, as well as bird lists. Boating can be difficult in this shallow lake, depending on water levels. The most popular driving route is the road around Pond 5, which is closed during hunting season (early September through early January).

Directions: *From Fairfield, drive 5 miles north on U.S. Highway 89.*

Ownership: FWP (406) 454-3441
Size: 11,350 acres   **Closest Town:** Fairfield

CHARLIE RUSSELL COUNTRY

The long-billed curlew once was a common sight across the plains until much of its native habitat fell to the plow. Montana's open plains still offer refuge to the curlew.
MICHAEL S. SAMPLE

43. GIANT SPRINGS STATE PARK

Description: *URBAN SITE.* An exceptional urban wildlife site, this park contains the largest freshwater spring in the United States, discharging nearly 400 million gallons of water per day into the Missouri River. It's a great place to see trout; the adjacent hatchery is even better. The Giant Springs fish hatchery has an excellent self-guided tour and a large outdoor show pond where visitors can feed 8- to 12-pound rainbow trout. The Missouri River section that flows past Giant Springs is shallow, swift, and one of the last to freeze, so it attracts extraordinary concentrations of waterfowl in the winter. In the summer, ducks, Canada geese, American white pelicans, and shorebirds are present. It's a top-notch birding site (over 150 species have been seen here), especially along the 0.5-mile trail that runs west from the springs along the river's edge. Look for bald eagles, common loons, and American dippers in the winter, and prairie falcons, gray partridges, ring-necked pheasants, gulls, and double-crested cormorants spring through fall. The visitor center (right across the roadway from the springs) features taxidermy mounts of grizzly and black bears, educational features on fish and bird recognition, wildlife photographs, and a mini-theater that shows wildlife videos. It's open 8 a.m. - 5 p.m. Monday through Friday (8 a.m. - 7 p.m. weekdays and 10 a.m. - 7 p.m. weekends in the summer).

Directions: In Great Falls, take River Road and turn north onto Giant Springs Road.

Ownership: FWP (406) 454-3441
Size: 260 acres   **Closest Town:** Great Falls

The hatchery adjacent to Giant Springs State Park is an excellent place to see large trout. The park is an exceptional birding area, with over 150 species recorded.
CRAIG & LIZ LARCOM

44. BENTON LAKE NATIONAL WILDLIFE REFUGE

Description: One of the most productive waterfowl refuges in the United States, this refuge is also one of the best places to see and photograph broods of ducks and geese. This easily accessible site provides a great opportunity to see a rich diversity of native prairie and wetland wildlife—it is an important stop for migrating waterfowl March through April and September through October, attracting ducks (up to 100,000), tundra swans (up to 4,000), and snow geese (up to 40,000). It's also recognized by the Western Hemisphere Shorebird Reserve Network as a significant area for migrating and nesting shorebirds. Nesting wetland birds include 12 species of ducks, assorted waders such as black-crowned night-herons and white-faced ibis, 3 species of gulls, and 3 kinds of terns. Native prairie wildlife includes chestnut-collared longspurs, grasshopper and savannah sparrows, upland sandpipers, burrowing owls, coyotes, badgers and white-tailed jackrabbits. Two auto tour routes are the best way to see the refuge. The 9-mile Prairie Marsh Drive has numbered signs corresponding to an interpretive brochure available at the main information sign. The Lower Marsh Road (open July 15 through September 30) is 4 miles long and self-interpreted. Check at the headquarters for other public use opportunities and regulations.

Directions: *Just north of Great Falls, turn off U.S. Highway 87 onto Bootlegger Trail (Secondary Route 225) and follow it 9 miles to the refuge entrance on the left side of road. From the turnoff, it's about 1.5 miles to the informational signs.*

Ownership: USFWS (406) 727-7400
Size: 12,383 acres   **Closest Town:** Great Falls

Thousands of snow geese fill the air at Benton Lake National Wildlife Refuge. Spectacular flights of snow geese also may be observed at Freezout Lake in the spring and fall. KRISTI DUBOIS

45. MISSOURI RIVER RECREATION ROAD

Description: This 35-mile, slow-paced driving alternative to Interstate 15 follows the Missouri River through rocky canyons and rolling prairie. Visitors often see American white pelicans, great blue herons, Canada geese, nesting wood ducks, and bald eagles, which are especially numerous in the winter. Look for a golden eagle nest at Eagle Rock, about 6 miles downstream from Craig. Other more frequently seen bird species include gulls (the black-headed ones are probably Franklin's gull), ducks, magpies, and bluebirds (look for bluebird houses on the fence posts). Deer and coyotes are common, black bears can sometimes be spotted, and beaver dams can be seen near the road on Little Prickly Pear Creek. The recreation road officially ends at Hardy Creek; drivers can continue north on the frontage road through Cascade and on to Ulm, along a notable spring migration route for hawks and eagles.

Directions: *The recreation road runs between Helena and Great Falls. From the south, take Interstate 15 Exit 219 at Little Spring; from the north, take Exit 247 at Hardy Creek.*

Ownership: PVT, FWP (406) 454-3441
Size: 35-mile drive   **Closest Town:** Cascade

Look for American white pelicans flying and swimming in formation along the Missouri River, as well as many of Montana's larger lakes and other rivers. They consume all types of fish, from suckers to trout. MICHAEL S. SAMPLE

46. LONESOME LAKE

Description: Lonesome Lake is a unique prairie wetland complex, heavily used in the past by American Indians. It has one of the highest concentrations of te-pee rings in Montana. (Remember, it is illegal to collect or disturb cultural re-sources.) The shortgrass prairie habitat in this complex is a wildlife oasis in a desert of cropland. The shallow lake provides a resting spot for migrating water-fowl and shorebirds, especially in the spring. Look for pintails, mallards, blue-winged teal, gadwalls, shovelers, willets, American avocets, and dowitchers. Oc-casionally tundra swans and snow geese have been spotted. South of the parking area, in shortgrass prairie habitat, watch for chestnut-collared and McCowan's longspurs, horned larks, and Swainson's hawks. In the summer, burrowing owls, pronghorn, coyotes, foxes, and badgers are present. In the fall and winter, rough-legged hawks, prairie falcons, and waterfowl can be observed. Since Lonesome Lake is a shallow prairie pothole, it is often dry by late summer unless rains have been especially plentiful. *NO FACILITIES. ROAD TO EDGE OF LAKE MAY BE IMPASSABLE IN WET WEATHER.*

Directions: *From U.S. Highway 87, turn west on Montana Highway 432 at Big Sandy. Travel west 4 miles, then turn right (north) onto a graveled county road and proceed 5.5 miles. Turn left (west) onto an undeveloped trail and proceed approxi-mately 0.33 mile to the edge of Lonesome Lake.*

Ownership: BLM (406) 265-5891
Size: 14,596 acres   **Closest Town:** Big Sandy

47. BEAVER CREEK COUNTY PARK

Description: This wild area is one of the largest county parks in the United States. A long, narrow corridor (about 17 miles long and 1 mile wide) it runs along the north slopes of the Bear Paw Mountains. Its good paved road passes through rolling grasslands, ponderosa pine forests, and aspen and cottonwood groves. Rocky cliffs and small ponds and lakes add to the scenic diversity. Birders can see warblers, vireos, soras, prairie falcons, Clark's nutcrackers, crossbills, and ring-necked pheasants, as well as species of special interest such as yellow-breasted chats and lazuli buntings along the creek. Watch for eagles just north of Daryl Marden Memorial on the scraggy butte. White-tailed and mule deer, elk, and bobcats also use the park, and coyotes and raccoons are plentiful. Springs provide open water for waterfowl in the winter; beaver dams are abundant near these areas. Beaver Creek is open in the winter to snowmo-biles and cross-country skiing. Further information is available at the park office at Camp Kiwanis, about 10 miles into the park, where wildlife watchers can pay the $5 user fee.

Directions: *In Havre, follow Fifth Avenue to Beaver Creek Road. Follow it for 9 miles to Beaver Creek County Park.*

Ownership: Hill County (406) 395-4565
Size: 10,000 acres   **Closest Town:** Havre

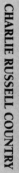

48. BR-12 PRAIRIE MARSH

Description: This 200-acre prairie marsh in the midst of open grasslands is narrow and long—nearly a mile in length—making for a pleasant walk. It's a great place to view ducks, Canada geese, golden eagles, ferruginous hawks, Swainson's hawks, shorebirds, and songbirds for much of the year. In the spring, look for goldeneyes, redheads, canvasbacks, and ring-necked ducks in the thick cattails at the north end, where there are also nesting structures for mallards. In the summer, broods of waterfowl are always present. Look for nesting waterfowl on the small islands. Muskrats, raccoons, and jackrabbits can be seen near the marsh, and pronghorn are common. Look for mule deer in the woody draw below the dam. BR-12 is a relatively remote site, with no restrictions on access. *NO FACILITIES. HIGH-CLEARANCE VEHICLE RECOMMENDED FOR UNPAVED ROAD TO RESERVOIR.*

Directions: *Take U.S. Highway 2 to Zurich and drive 0.5 mile west of town to Zurich County Road. Turn north and travel 9 miles to an unimproved dirt road on the east. Visitors can either walk or drive a high-clearance vehicle on the road a short distance to reach the reservoir.*

Ownership: BLM (406) 265-5891
Size: 1,800 acres   **Closest Town:** Zurich

Mule deer are the most common deer in Montana. They are found in virtually every habitat type. In many parts of Charlie Russell Country, mule deer may be seen in agricultural areas, especially at dawn and dusk. MICHAEL S. SAMPLE

Description: This 149-mile section of the Missouri River is the only major portion that has been preserved in a natural, free-flowing state. It provides a remarkable float trip for canoers and rafters, suitable for beginners. Along the way, habitats change from grasslands to beautiful white cliffs to badlands. The Evans Bend area starts at river mile 6 on the south side (use your BLM floater's guide) and continues for 2 miles through a dense forest of mature cottonwoods that supports deer, wild turkeys, Canada geese, and a great blue heron rookery, as well as 200+ species of song birds. Access to this area is difficult except by river. At river mile 21, the Marias River flows into the Missouri; the large riparian area (the Richard E. Wood Wildlife Area) is a good place to take a hike. (This BLM-owned area is also accessible from U.S. Highway 87.) Look for Canada geese nesting on the bluffs, white-tailed deer, gray partridge, ring-necked pheasants, and sharp-tailed grouse. The steep rock walls near Eagle Creek (river mile 56) are a good place to look for nesting raptors (especially prairie falcons) and cliff swallows; Canada geese and American white pelicans float the river in the summer. Judith Landing (river mile 88.5) also has a heron rookery and is a good place to see eagles, songbirds, and waterfowl. At Holmes Rapid (river mile 91.5), walk along the south side of the river to the sagebrush flat to see a 200-acre prairie dog town, and possibly burrowing owls and coyotes. Near Greasewood Bottom (river mile 109), the ridges and coulees often contain bighorn sheep and mule deer, especially in the fall. Near Woodhawk Bottom and Cow Island (river miles 127-131), walk riparian areas and badlands to see both mule and white-tailed deer, ring-necked pheasants, Canada geese, American white pelicans, and beavers. In the Two Calf area (river miles 143-145), look for the prairie elk herd inhabiting the river bottoms of the Charles M. Russell National Wildlife Refuge, and for bighorn sheep. *RIVER MAPS AVAILABLE FROM THE BUREAU OF LAND MANAGEMENT.*

Directions: *Take Montana Highway 80 to Fort Benton, the start of the Wild and Scenic portion of the Missouri River. The Fred Robinson Bridge, where U.S. Highway 191 crosses the Missouri northeast of Lewistown, marks the end.*

Ownership: BLM (406) 538-7461
Size: 149-mile stretch of river   **Closest Town:** Fort Benton

CHARLIE RUSSELL COUNTRY

How high can a bird fly? The typical elevation is between 5,000 and 20,000 feet, but a flock of swans was once seen by an airline pilot at 29,000 feet.

50. SQUARE BUTTE

Description: Scenic Square Butte is a volcanic landmark rising some 1,700 feet from the plains of north-central Montana. It has exceptional wildlife values. Deer, pronghorn, and sometimes elk can be seen near the butte, and a herd of about 80 mountain goats can consistently be seen on top. The butte's steep cliffs provide outstanding nesting habitat for raptors; there's a high density of breeding prairie falcons here, as well as golden eagles, and hawks. Access to Square Butte is available only through the good will of the private landowner, so please be especially courteous. There are instructions and a check-in box at the ranch gate; visitors must ask permission. The road to the butte is closed during hunting season and is sometimes closed during wet weather. The unmarked 1-mile hike from the end of the road to the top of the butte is quite steep but well worth the view; it takes about an hour.

Directions: *Take Montana Highway 80 to the town of Square Butte, then drive west on a county road for 2.5 miles, following the signs to Square Butte Natural Area. Access to the butte is through the headquarters of a private ranch. Park at the base of the butte and then hike about 1 mile to reach the top.*

Ownership: PVT, BLM (406) 538-7461
Size: 3,000 acres   **Closest Town:** Square Butte

A ferruginous hawk guards her four chicks in their nest along a cliff. Steep, rocky landmarks such as Square Butte provide importanat nesting sites for raptors on the open plains. Please avoid approaching nest sites, as ferruginous hawks are extremely sensitive to human disturbance. KRISTI DUBOIS

51. JUDITH RIVER WILDLIFE MANAGEMENT AREA

Description: With rolling grasslands and ponderosa pine forests, this area serves as a wintering ground for elk and deer from the adjacent Big Belt Mountains. The Wildlife Management Area looks into steep, forested canyons with rocky outcroppings. Coyotes, red foxes, long-tailed weasels, badgers, and bobcats are other common mammals. Nearly 100 bird species have been recorded here, including raptors such as golden eagles, Swainson's hawks, goshawks, and great horned owls. Also frequently seen are Clark's nutcrackers, Lewis' woodpeckers, bluebirds, and western tanagers. Primary access to the WMA is via the road that bisects it. Hiking is possible anywhere in summer and fall. On the approach to the WMA, look for birds (especially warblers and vireos), beavers, and waterfowl in the streamside vegetation along the Judith River. WMA open to fall hunting. *LAND ALONG RIVER IS PRIVATE; VIEW FROM ROADSIDES ONLY. NO FACILITIES. WMA CLOSED DECEMBER 1 THROUGH MAY 14; VIEWING AT THIS TIME IS LIMITED TO THE ROAD.*

Directions: *From Lewistown, take U.S. Highway 87 west to Hobson, then take Secondary Route 239 west to Utica. From Utica, follow the gravel road 12 miles to the south, then turn right onto Yogo Creek Road (after Sapphire Village) and proceed 1.3 miles to the WMA.*

Ownership: FWP (406) 454-3441
Size: 5,000 acres   **Closest Town:** Utica

52. BIG SPRINGS TROUT HATCHERY

Description: This state hatchery on beautiful Big Spring Creek provides cutthroat, rainbow, and brown trout, and kokanee salmon to locations all over Montana. The hatchery holds its maximum number of fish in the spring—up to 3.5 million at that time. The show pond features albino rainbow trout and fish as large as 15 pounds. Take short walks around the hatchery to see Big Spring Creek rising from the ground and to see waterfowl (look for wood ducks in the summer), white-tailed deer, muskrats, beavers, eagles, and belted kingfishers. Viewing is open from daylight to dusk year-round.

Directions: *In Lewistown, take First Avenue South. Follow for about 7 miles south and turn left at the second hatchery sign.*

Ownership: FWP (406) 538-5588
Size: 22.6 acres   **Closest Town:** Lewistown

REGION FOUR:
YELLOWSTONE COUNTRY

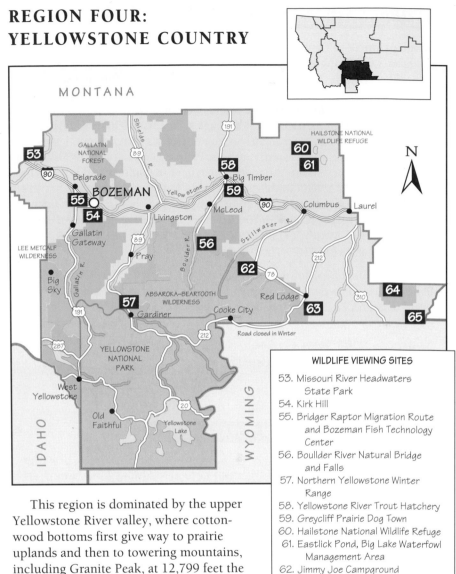

WILDLIFE VIEWING SITES

53. Missouri River Headwaters
    State Park
54. Kirk Hill
55. Bridger Raptor Migration Route
    and Bozeman Fish Technology
    Center
56. Boullder River Natural Bridge
    and Falls
57. Northern Yellowstone Winter
    Range
58. Yellowstone River Trout Hatchery
59. Greycliff Prairie Dog Town
60. Hailstone National Wildlife Refuge
61. Eastlick Pond, Big Lake Waterfowl
    Management Area
62. Jimmy Joe Campground
63. Meeteetse Trail
64. Pryor Mountains
65. Bad Pass Road

This region is dominated by the upper Yellowstone River valley, where cottonwood bottoms first give way to prairie uplands and then to towering mountains, including Granite Peak, at 12,799 feet the highest mountain in Montana. The Northern Yellowstone Winter Range, just north of Yellowstone National Park, shelters one of the largest and most diverse groups of large grazing mammals in the lower 48 states. Open hillsides above the Yellowstone River provide winter habitat for elk, bighorn sheep, pronghorn, and mule deer. The high plateaus and canyons of the Pryor Mountains are home to elk, raptors, hundreds of bird species, even wild horses. The three forks of the Missouri River—the Madison, Jefferson and Gallatin rivers—come together at historic Missouri Headwaters State Park, where great horned owls, warblers, and painted turtles thrive in rich bottomlands and riparian areas.

53. MISSOURI HEADWATERS STATE PARK

Description: Made famous by the Lewis and Clark expedition, this state park lies where the Madison, Jefferson, and Gallatin Rivers join to form the Missouri River. The park has extensive cottonwood river bottoms and dry, rocky uplands that give way to limestone cliffs. The Headwaters Trail is a favorite birding site; in the summer, look for Canada geese with goslings, nesting osprey, nighthawks, rock wrens, magpies, lazuli buntings, northern orioles, white-throated swifts, and an abundance of warblers and vireos. There are great blue heron and double-crested cormorant rookeries on the Gallatin River, less than a mile upstream from where the rivers join. A hike up Lewis Rock or Fort Rock provides a great view and a good chance to see golden eagles, which nest on nearby cliffs. Prairie falcons are seen frequently. Marmots and Richardson's ground squirrels can be seen near the rocks, while in the meadows white-tailed deer are common and moose are occasionally seen. Coyotes are heard frequently at night. Although river otters are shy and elusive, their sign can be found nearby. Beavers and painted turtles are common and rattlesnakes, bull snakes, garter snakes, and racers all dwell here. Interpretive displays feature area wildlife and history. A canoe trip is a great way to see the area. No day-use fees for Montana residents.

Directions: *From Interstate 90, exit at Three Forks. Turn east on Secondary Route 205, then turn north on Secondary Route 286 and follow for 3 miles.*

Ownership: FWP (406) 994-4042
Size: 533 acres   **Closest Town:** Three Forks

Beaver dams create important habitat for a variety of wildlife, including fish, waterfowl, shorebirds, and even moose. Beavers are common along many streams and rivers in western Montana.   MICHAEL S. SAMPLE

54. KIRK HILL

Description: *URBAN SITE.* This hillside area, managed by the Museum of the Rockies, is a good spot to view wildlife and learn about natural history. There are some excellent signs identifying plants and trees. The area offers both short birding walks and longer hikes on adjacent Gallatin National Forest lands. The main trail starts out in a creek bottom area that's loaded with songbirds. It then climbs very steeply for 0.25 mile into dry, Douglas-fir-covered foothills, where loop trails from 0.3 to 0.6 mile in length originate. (Trail maps are posted at the entrance and at each trail intersection.) Near the southeast corner of the area hikers can hook up with a national forest trail to the Bozeman Creek/Hyalite Creek divide. More than 70 bird species have been recorded in the area; some birds of special interest include Steller's jays, Clark's nutcrackers, lazuli buntings, northern pygmy-owls, MacGillivray's warblers, Lincoln's sparrows, and great gray owls. Mule deer, elk, and moose are seen occasionally, and black bears use the area. It's a great area for wildflowers, many of which are identified by signs. *NO FACILITIES. PETS, HORSES, BICYCLES, HUNTING PROHIBITED.*

Directions: *From Bozeman, follow South 19th Avenue directly south for about 5 miles. As you approach the mountains, the road bears sharply to the right (west); Kirk Hill is on the south side of this sharp curve.*

Ownership: Montana State University (406) 994-5257
Size: 50 acres **Closest Town:** Bozeman

The irridescent colors of the Steller's jay are a familiar sight in the coniferous forests of Montana. MICHAEL S. SAMPLE

55. BRIDGER RAPTOR MIGRATION ROUTE AND BOZEMAN FISH TECHNOLOGY CENTER

Description: A major raptor migration route follows the Bridger Mountain Range; spectacular views of the Gallatin Valley and the surrounding mountains can be seen from the top of Bridger Bowl Ski Area. Every autumn, migrating hawks, falcons, and eagles fly south along the narrow backbone of the Bridger Range, taking advantage of rising thermal air currents. The route is the largest known flyway for golden eagles in the United States. At least 16 other species have been spotted from the observation platform here, but the most common are golden and bald eagles, northern harriers, sharp-shinned hawks, Cooper's hawks, red-tailed hawks, rough-legged hawks, and American kestrels. Other species occasionally seen include goshawks, merlins, peregrine and prairie falcons, and osprey. Hawkwatch International and the Gallatin National Forest in cooperation with Bridger Bowl Ski Area, maintain a migration monitoring station at the site September 10 through October 30; personnel are available to help people identify birds. The best viewing is 11 a.m. - 5 p.m. from September 24 through October 14. The hike to the monitoring station is extremely steep and takes about 2 hours. On the road to the raptor site, stop off at the Bozeman Fish Technology Center in Bridger Canyon on Montana Highway 86, where there are probably a wider variety of land birds than at any other similar-sized site in Montana. On a 0.25-mile trail along Bridger Creek look for American dippers, soras, killdeer, and spotted sandpipers; along the brushy banks of the stream and ravine look for Swainson's thrushes, warbling vireos, orange-crowned warblers, and American redstarts. Operated by the U.S. Fish and Wildlife Service, the Fish Technology Center is open 8 a.m. - 4 p.m. daily for self-guided tours. *TWO-HOUR HIKE TO VIEWING PLATFORM IS STRENUOUS, STEEP. BE PREPARED FOR STRONG WINDS AND INCLEMENT WEATHER. NO FACILITIES ON MOUNTAINTOP.*

Directions: *From Bozeman, take Montana Highway 86 north 16 miles following signs to Bridger Bowl Ski Area. Turn off at Bridger Bowl and follow the main road staying right of the lodge and parking area. Follow a winding gravel road to a Forest Service gate. Ahead is the Bridger ski lift; walk up the ski run until you cross a dirt maintenance road, then follow the switchback trail up to the head of the lift. Find the footpath just northwest of the lift operator's building and follow it up Bridger Ridge. There is a viewing platform 200 feet north of a small building. The Fish Technology Center is farther down Bridger Canyon, 4 miles north of Bozeman on MT 86.*

Ownership: PVT; USFWS (406) 587-9265; USFS (406) 587-6920
Size: NA   **Closest Town:** Bozeman

Owls are truly masters of the night. Some owls can hunt down prey illuminated by the equivalent of one candle placed 390 yards away. This visual acuity is 50 times greater than human night vision.

56. BOULDER RIVER NATURAL BRIDGE AND FALLS

Description: A 70-foot-high waterfall plunges into a deep pool below the remnant of a natural arch bridge (once spanning the river) at this spectacular limestone canyon area along the Boulder River. Outside the canyon walls are foothills of open Douglas-fir and limber pine forests broken by sagebrush and grassland. In the immediate distance is the Absaroka-Beartooth Wilderness. There are 2 trails on either side of the canyon above Boulder River Falls. The northside trail is a 0.25-mile paved loop trail with interpretive signs. The second trail crosses a wooden footbridge suspended over the river and dead-ends after 0.25 mile. Both trails offer good opportunities to see migratory birds in the summer—western tanagers, warbling vireos, mountain bluebirds, violet-green swallows, and Townsend's solitaires. Golden eagles nest in the area and can be seen year-round. In the fall, black bears are common, as are yellow-bellied marmots, yellow-pine chipmunks, red squirrels, and mule and white-tailed deer. In the winter, look for elk, mule deer, and rough-legged hawks. An interpretive sign explains elk winter use in the area. Two miles past the natural bridge and waterfall is the Main Boulder Station, another good place to view songbirds. Grouse Creek Trail #14 leads from the station and is an excellent hike through quaking aspen and Douglas-fir forests; look for elk, mule deer, black bears, and a variety of birds, including ruffed grouse, white-throated swifts, and red crossbills. The trail is moderately difficult and ends 7 miles to the west at the West Boulder Campground.

Directions: *From Interstate 90 at Big Timber, go 25 miles southwest on Secondary Route 298 following the main Boulder River. The site is 0.25 mile within the Gallatin National Forest boundary.*

Ownership: USFS (406) 932-5155
Size: 40 acres; 0.25- and 7-mile trails   **Closest Town:** Big Timber

The beautiful western tanager belongs to a group of birds known to scientists as "neotropical migrants." These are birds that breed in North America, but winter south of the Mexico-United States border. Declining populations of neotropical migrants have become a serious concern.
DONALD M. JONES

Description: Passing through winter range of the largest and most diverse group of hoofed animals in the lower 48 states, this drive route goes through parts of the Gallatin National Forest and Yellowstone National Park. The scenic route offers rugged mountains and grassy foothills. Between December and May, the range is the major wintering area for the Northern Yellowstone elk herd, which at about 20,000 is the world's largest. Mule deer, pronghorn, and an occasional bison (straying outside Park boundaries) add diversity. In the winter, bighorn sheep are often found ranging from the Devil's Slide turnout to Cinnabar Mountain, right across the Yellowstone River at Corwin Springs on the grassy slopes. A 3-panel exhibit at the Devil's Slide turnout interprets the migration of wildlife and the efforts to safeguard a winter range corridor outside the Park. The Yellowstone River between Corwin Springs and Gardiner is also an important wintering area for bald eagles; look for their white heads in the tallest trees and snags.

Directions: *This 15-mile drive route begins on U.S. Highway 89, about 15 miles north of Gardiner at a U.S. Forest Service interpretive display on cutthroat trout, and extends south to the town of Gardiner. At Corwin Springs, follow either U.S. 89 or cross the Yellowstone River and take a gravel road to Gardiner. The Northern Yellowstone Winter Range extends another 42 miles from Gardiner through Yellowstone National Park (south to Mammoth Hot Springs, then east towards Cooke City).*

Ownership: PVT, State of MT, Yellowstone National Park, USFS (406) 848-7375
Size: 58-mile stretch   **Closest Town:** Gardiner

The open hillsides above the Yellowstone River near Gardiner provide critical winter range for elk and many other species. Excessive disturbance of these animals on their winter ranges can cause them to expend energy otherwise needed to make it through the winter. CHRISTOPHER CAUBLE

58. YELLOWSTONE RIVER TROUT HATCHERY

Description: This brood hatchery for Yellowstone cutthroat trout maintains adult fish (brood) from which eggs are taken to supply production hatcheries (those that raise fish). It's an exceptional place for viewing trout, with 3 outside raceways that can have 2,500 or more fish during the summer. The largest fish are 18 to 26 inches long and can weigh up to 6 pounds. It's particularly interesting to visit between March and May when the eggs are removed. On Tuesdays the fish are checked for "ripe" eggs; on Wednesdays the eggs are stripped from the fish. The hatchery produces about 1.5 million eggs each year. Each 4-year-old female trout produces about 3,000 eggs annually. During the summer months, inside raceways contain 400,000 to 600,000 fry. In August most of these 2- to 3-inch fish are deposited via helicopters and airplanes into high mountain lakes. The hatchery is open 7 days a week 8 a.m. - 4:30 p.m.; staff are on hand to answer questions and to lead tours. (School groups are welcome.) A pamphlet about the hatchery is available. In summer, the outdoor raceways are left open for evening viewing. Watch for belted kingfishers seeking an easy meal. Behind the hatchery is a small, state-owned wetland that has red-winged blackbird colonies, great blue herons, waterfowl, and white-tail deer.

Directions: From Interstate 90, take either Big Timber exit and head to the town center. Turn north on McLeod Street (the main street) and follow for 0.5 mile to the hatchery. (Cross railroad tracks and go down a hill).

Ownership: FWP (406) 932-4434
Size: 8 acres   **Closest Town:** Big Timber

59. GREYCLIFF PRAIRIE DOG TOWN

Description: A barrier-free site, Greycliff is one of the most accessible prairie dog viewing areas in Montana. Primarily shortgrass prairie and sagebrush, the town is usually teeming with black-tailed prairie dogs. Interpretive panels at the parking area explain prairie dog ecology and behavior. Photo opportunities are exceptional. Please refrain from feeding praire dogs—handouts can damage their digestive systems and subvert their natural behavior. Red-tailed hawks and golden eagles sometimes fly over, looking for a meal, and common prairie songbirds such as western meadowlarks, vesper sparrows, horned larks, and mountain bluebirds frequently are seen nearby. Prairie dogs usually are less active November through early March, but can be dependably seen the rest of the year unless the weather is excessively cold or hot. View from the road or parking area.

Directions: From Interstate 90, take Exit 377 about 7 miles east of Big Timber. From there, follow the signs to the viewing site on the south side of I-90.

Ownership: FWP (406) 252-4654
Size: 98 acres   **Closest Town:** Big Timber

60. HAILSTONE NATIONAL WILDLIFE REFUGE

Description: A large alkaline lake, the Hailstone refuge is in wide-open short-grass prairie country dominated by rocky outcroppings and small grassy hills. This medium-sized refuge is noted primarily for its waterfowl (several thousand during migration times) and shorebirds, commonly including mallards, gadwalls, teals, redheads, canvasbacks, American avocets, phalaropes, American white pelicans, grebes, and gulls. A good place to view water birds is a small hill that overlooks the lake. Several mudflats near the lake are a good spot for shorebirds. Pronghorn and sharp-tailed grouse are frequently seen in the upland areas, which are vegetated with sagebrush, greasewood, and native grasses. There is a black-tailed prairie dog town on the east side of the lake; watch for golden eagles, burrowing owls, and hawks preying on the dogs. Peregrine falcons also have been sighted here. *MOTORIZED BOATS PROHIBITED ON LAKE.*

Directions: *At Columbus, take Secondary Route 306 to Rapelje. From Rapelje, turn east on a county road and follow for 4 miles to Hailstone Basin Road. Take this gravel road north about 1.5 miles to the refuge.*

Ownership: USFWS (406) 538-8706
Size: 1,913 acres   **Closest Town:** Rapelje

Prairie dogs have a highly-developed social structure. In this photo, a prairie dog serving as lookout gives an "all-clear" signal. Prairie dog towns are a hub of wildlife activity, providing habitat for dozens of other species, including uncommon wildlife such as the mountain plover, ferruginous hawk, swift fox, and the black-footed ferret, a federally-listed endangered species. HARRY ENGELS

YELLOWSTONE COUNTRY

71

61. EASTLICK POND/BIG LAKE WATERFOWL MANAGEMENT AREA

Description: Eastlick Pond, easily visible from a fair dirt road, is a productive prairie pothole popular with Billings-area birders. The pond is privately owned and viewing is restricted to roadsides. Chestnut-collared longspurs, horned larks, water pipits, western meadowlarks, red-tailed hawks, northern harriers, and gulls can often be seen here. Waterfowl commonly viewed include American wigeons, mallards, and teal. It's also a concentration spot for great blue herons and Canada geese in the spring and fall. Shorebirds seen here include sandpipers and long-billed curlews. There's a black-tailed prairie dog town across the road from the pond, a dependable place to see nesting burrowing owls in the summer. (Also look near the top of the hill on the same side of the road as the pond.) The shelterbelt of trees 2 miles north of the pond often holds small birds such as warblers, Say's phoebe, American goldfinch, and ruby-crowned kinglet. Big Lake is a large alkaline lake that's a great place to see ducks, geese, and shorebirds—when there's water. In wet years it's usually good for American white pelicans and tundra swans during migration as well as cormorants and gulls. Shorebirds found here include black-necked stilts, black-bellied plovers, yellowlegs, American avocets, and phalaropes. It's a good place for the unusual—look for scoters and peregrine falcons. In late April or early May birders often see more than 50 bird species on the drive to these sites. *NO FACILITIES. ROADS MAY BE UNPASSABLE WHEN WET.*

Directions: *From Billings, follow Rimrock Road to Secondary Route 302, then drive toward Molt, approximately 21 miles. Just before reaching Molt, turn left (due west) on the dirt road (Eastlick Road) and follow for about 2 miles. Turn right onto Lakeview Road and proceed 0.75 mile to a small pond on the right (known to local birders as Corral Pond). To reach Big Lake, continue north on Lakeview Road until its intersection with the Molt-Rapelje road. Turn left (west) on this road and drive 4.7 miles. At an old grain elevator, turn left (Wheat Basin Road) and drive another 1.1 miles to Big Lake (9.1 miles from Eastlick Pond).*

Ownership: PVT, FWP (406) 252-4654
Size: Eastlick Pond, 20 acres; Big Lake, 2,800 acres
Closest Town: Molt

Abundant wildflowers at Jimmy Joe Campground attract a variety of butterflies, including this pale tiger swallowtail.
MICHAEL S. SAMPLE

62. JIMMY JOE CAMPGROUND

Description: The profusion of spring and summer wildflowers at this picturesque campground near the rugged Beartooth Mountains and East Rosebud River attracts an array of butterflies. An interpretive sign describes butterfly ecology, habitats, and viewing hints. In May and early June, look for a large bed of the kinnikinnick plant (close to the ground with green, shiny leaves) where the campground road joins the main road at the south end. This plant provides nectar for hairstreak, elfin, and blue butterflies. In June, mourning cloak, Weidemeyer's admiral, angle wing, and blue butterflies can be found patrolling the campground road. In late June and July the pink dogbane flowers lining the paved canyon road provide nectar for about 20 species of butterflies and skippers. Later in the year there are fewer species, but visitors can still find angle wings, sulfurs, and lesser fritillaries, and a new crop of mourning cloaks. Mule and white-tailed deer, black bears, and moose are sometimes seen near the road, and the campground itself is a good birding area.

Directions: *Take Montana Highway 78 to Roscoe, then follow signs to East Rosebud Lake for about 9 miles south on a gravel road. Jimmy Joe Campground and the interpretive display is about 5 miles before the lake and is well marked with signs.*

Ownership: USFS (406) 446-2103
Size: 10 acres   **Closest Town:** Roscoe

63. MEETEETSE TRAIL

Description: The habitats along this drive route change dramatically from river bottom to mountains to arid prairie, and feature large rock spires, rolling foothills with aspen groves, willow-edged ponds, and near-desert sagebrush flats. Wildlife viewing here is equally diverse. Look for beavers, white-tailed deer, moose, and a variety of songbirds along the first 4 miles of the trail immediately after crossing Rock Creek. Mule deer and an occasional black bear can be seen where the trail climbs into more mountainous habitat; golden eagles and red-tailed hawks often soar overhead. Moving into the drier prairie, look for coyotes, foxes, and badgers. Sage grouse and pronghorn can be seen on the sagebrush flats. There are trails along the North and South Forks of Grove Creek, and hiking is possible on nearby public land. The road isn't plowed in the winter, but cross-country skiing is a good way to see the area (snow permitting). The northern portions of the road pass through deer and elk winter range. Mountain bicycling also has excellent potential in season. *NO FACILITIES.*

Directions: *From Red Lodge, drive 1 mile south on U.S. Highway 212. Just before you reach the Forest Service ranger station, take a dirt road going southeast. This is the start of the 19-mile drive route, which ends where Meeteetse Trail hits Secondary Route 72 south of Belfry. Note: about a mile from the turnoff after crossing Rock Creek, bear left and proceed up the hill.*

Ownership: PVT, BLM (406) 657-6262
Size: 19-mile drive   **Closest Town:** Red Lodge

64. PRYOR MOUNTAINS

Description: Drivers who take this scenic route will pass through high plateaus, spectacular canyons, and thick Douglas-fir forests. There's good birding along Sage Creek and in the canyons; look for sage thrashers, American kestrels, rock wrens, ruby-crowned kinglets, and warblers. Sage Creek Campground is notable for both hummingbirds and green-tailed towhees. Near the Big Ice Cave (take Forest Road 849 off Forest Road 3085), look for bats roosting along the limestone cliffs. There's a small bighorn sheep herd here, too, but it's infrequently seen. The drive ends at Dry Head Vista, a barren plateau with a stunning view that's a good place to see raptors—especially golden eagles. Hikers can go anywhere along the route; for an interesting short walk, drive down the Crooked Creek Road (FR 3085) until it hits Wyoming Creek. From here, a 10-minute walk on an unmarked trail following Wyoming Creek gives a good all-around view of the area. For a longer hike, take Forest Road 3092 south off FR 3085 just west of the Big Ice Cave. Drive the couple miles along a 2-track road, then park and hike along Commissary Ridge for a great view of the Pryor Mountains Wild Horse Range to the east. Roads here are impassable in wet weather. High-clearance vehicles are helpful year-round, and a map is essential. This is remote country, so take caution. *VIEWING ROUTE CROSSES CROW INDIAN RESERVATION; A TRESPASS PERMIT IS REQUIRED FOR ANYONE WHO WISHES TO EXIT THEIR VEHICLE WHILE ON RESERVATION LANDS. PERMITS MAY BE OBTAINED FROM THE CROW TRIBAL AGENCY LOCATED IN CROW AGENCY; CALL (406) 638-2850. PICK UP A MAP OF THE PRYOR MOUNTAINS FROM FOREST SERVICE OFFICES IN BILLINGS OR RED LODGE.*

Directions: *See map below. From Bridger, take U.S. Highway 310 south for about 2 miles. Turn left (east) onto Pryor Mountain Road and proceed about 15 miles to Sage Creek. Continue east along Sage Creek on Forest Road 3085; from here it's about 7 miles to the Sage Creek Campground. This drive extends from Sage Creek Campground to the Dry Head Vista, about 12 miles. Follow FR 3085 for about 6 miles east of Sage Creek Campground, then take a left onto Forest Road 849 for about another 6 miles.*

Ownership: Crow Indian Reservation, USFS (406) 446-2103
Size: 77,000 acres **Closest Town:** Bridger

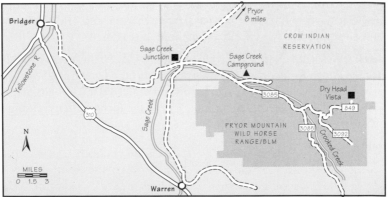

74

65. BAD PASS ROAD

Description: Bighorn Canyon is Montana's most spectacular canyon area, with colorful cliffs up to 2,000 feet high and expanses of prairie grasslands. The Bad Pass Road is a 25-mile drive route on a paved highway that passes through the 30,000-acre Pryor Mountain Wild Horse Range. Sanctuary for 121 wild horses, it is jointly managed by the National Park Service and Bureau of Land Management. In the fall and spring, bighorn sheep are often visible close to the road, especially near the Devil Canyon Overlook. Mule deer and raptors are common residents of the canyon, as are over 200 bird species. The Bighorn Canyon Visitor Center near Lovell has maps of the park as well as exhibits. Hiking is possible almost anywhere; a good bet is the trail that starts behind the Layout Creek Ranger Station. It passes through a juniper woodland area leading into a canyon and a natural spring, and is a good place to see both wild horses and bighorn sheep. Another great way to see the canyon and its wildlife is a boat ride tour that leaves from Horseshoe Bend.

Directions: *Take U.S. Highway 310 south to Lovell, Wyoming, then follow U.S. Highway 14A a short distance until it joins Wyoming Highway 37. Turn north onto WY 37 (Bad Pass Trail). This is the start of the 25-mile drive route, which ends at Barry's Landing.*

Ownership: NPS (307) 548-2251
Size: 120,000 acres; 25-mile drive   **Closest Town:** Lovell, Wyoming

Certain types of wildlife viewing demand caution. Rattlesnakes may be encountered in many areas, but especially around rocky outcroppings in central and eastern Montana. By helping to keep rodent populations in check, they play an important role in the prairie environment.   HANK FISCHER

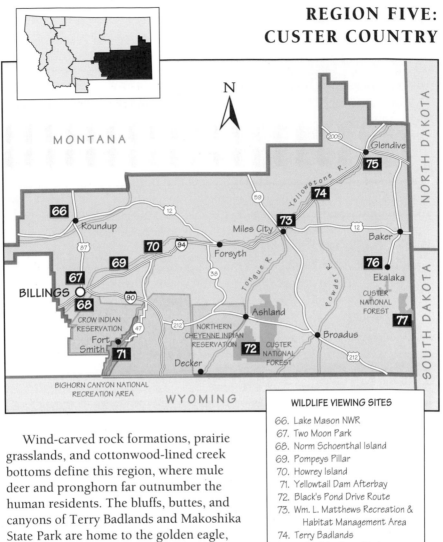

N

MONTANA

NORTH DAKOTA

SOUTH DAKOTA

Glendive

75

74

Roundup

66

Miles City

73

Baker

70

Forsyth

69

76

Ekalaka

BILLINGS

67

68

CROW INDIAN
RESERVATION

Fort
Smith

71

NORTHERN
CHEYENNE INDIAN
RESERVATION

Ashland

72

CUSTER
NATIONAL
FOREST

Broadus

CUSTER
NATIONAL
FOREST

77

Decker

BIGHORN CANYON NATIONAL
RECREATION AREA

WYOMING

WILDLIFE VIEWING SITES
66. Lake Mason NWR
67. Two Moon Park
68. Norm Schoenthal Island
69. Pompeys Pillar
70. Howrey Island
71. Yellowtail Dam Afterbay
72. Black's Pond Drive Route
73. Wm. L. Matthews Recreation &
    Habitat Management Area
74. Terry Badlands
75. Makoshika State Park
76. Medicine Rocks State Park
77. Long Pines

Wind-carved rock formations, prairie grasslands, and cottonwood-lined creek bottoms define this region, where mule deer and pronghorn far outnumber the human residents. The bluffs, buttes, and canyons of Terry Badlands and Makoshika State Park are home to the golden eagle, prairie falcon, a variety of snakes, and the jackrabbit. Custer Country is more than prairie lands. The ponderosa pine and aspen draws of Long Pines shelter the greatest concentration of nesting merlins in the U.S. Two Moon Park, in the rich cottonwood bottomlands of the Yellowstone River, is a birding hotspot near the metropolis of Billings, with over 200 species identified.

66. LAKE MASON NATIONAL WILDLIFE REFUGE

Description: The reeds, cattails, and mudflats of this extensive prairie marsh attract nesting populations of waterfowl, including mallards, gadwalls, teal, and pintails. Also seen are a great variety of shorebirds, such as yellowlegs, avocets, phalaropes, upland sandpipers, and willets—except during very dry years. Migrating Canada geese, gulls, and American white pelicans can be seen in the spring and fall, along with the occasional bald eagle and peregrine falcon. Several pronghorn herds roam the uplands around the lake, and a black-tailed prairie dog town can be found along its southeastern edge. Burrowing owls use the dog holes for their nests. Prairie rattlesnakes and horned lizards can also be seen here. A portion of the refuge (primarily the north and east sections) is closed to public access, but the rest of the refuge is open to hiking and non-motorized boating. *HIGH-CLEARANCE OR FOUR-WHEEL-DRIVE VEHICLE RECOMMENDED.*

Directions: *From Roundup, take U.S. 87 (Main Street) to 13th Avenue. Turn west and follow for 1 block, then turn west onto Golf Course Road. Follow this road for 6.5 miles, then turn right and proceed north for about 3 miles.*

Ownership: USFWS (406) 538-8706
Size: 16,830 acres   **Closest Town:** Roundup

67. TWO MOON PARK

Description: *URBAN SITE.* This Yellowstone River park is a top birding spot, with over 200 species recorded. The river bottom habitat includes cottonwood trees and dense underbrush interspersed with backwater sloughs. A slough along the north side of the park is a dependable place to see waterfowl and beavers, with thick vegetation allowing a stealthy approach. View nesting wood ducks in spring and summer and waterfowl of all kinds in the winter, since the slough usually doesn't freeze. Look for bald eagles in the winter and spring; migrating warblers (including Townsend's, Nashville, and blackpoll), orioles, common yellowthroats, and black-headed grosbeaks also appear in spring. Screech owls and great horned owls nest in the park, and Canada geese and American white pelicans ply the river. Mammals include white-tailed and mule deer, raccoons, and red foxes. Several unmarked trails crisscross the area, and a designated nature trail with 6 marked posts circles the park. Cross-country skiing is possible. A brochure describing the nature trail is available at the caretaker's home. The park is open from a half-hour before sunrise to 10 p.m.

Directions: *In Billings, take U.S. Highway 87 (Main Street) north, passing Metra. Just after the Airport Road intersection (0.2 mile), turn right on Lake Elmo Road. This becomes Bench Boulevard. Drive 0.6 mile and turn right onto Two Moon Road; follow the road a short distance to the park.*

Ownership: Yellowstone County (406) 256-2701
Size: 150 acres   **Closest Town:** Billings

Thoreau called the mountain bluebird "the bird that carries the sky on its back." This songbird usually relies on tree cavities for nesting, but in many open areas of Montana, bird houses have been placed on fences to attract these insect eaters. STEVE WIRT

68. NORM SCHOENTHAL ISLAND

Description: *URBAN SITE.* Bounded on the south by the Yellowstone River and on the north and east by Barbara's Slough, an old river channel, this 120-acre island is a great place to see a variety of wildlife close to town. The island's prevailing cottonwood trees are scattered and young, so the forest beneath them is open. Much of the island is covered by grass, and dense willow thickets and brush can be found along the water courses and pooling areas. Barbara's Oxbow, a shallow lake near the river, has abundant reeds and cattails and is a good place to see turtles and leopard frogs. Here, and along the nearby river sandbars, a variety of smaller shorebirds such as killdeer, greater and lesser yellowlegs, and solitary and spotted sandpipers can be seen. Along the river, look for bald eagles during winter and spring. During warmer months, be alert for Canada geese nesting on the islands and gravel bars, and American white pelicans, great blue herons, double-breasted cormorants and several species of ducks, including common mergansers and common goldeneyes feeding in the backwaters and along the main channel. California and ring-billed gulls may be seen in considerable numbers. White-tailed deer, cottontail rabbits, porcupines, skunks, foxes, and other mammals live in the grassy glades and brush, while fox squirrels share the forest canopy with downy woodpeckers and northern flickers. Migratory songbirds such as cedar waxwings, black-headed grosbeaks, and robins are common. Occasionally, a great horned owl is seen. Barbara's Slough is home to muskrats, raccoons, and beavers; girdled and fallen trees along the banks and dams in the channel testify to beaver activity.

Directions: *In Billings, take South Billings Boulevard (County Road 416) south 0.4 mile past the I-90 interchange. Turn right onto a dirt road and proceed southwest for 0.3 mile to Wendel's Bridge over Barbara's Slough. Proceed on foot across the bridge to Dutcher Trail, a 2.5-mile pathway that loops around the island. The left fork of the trail, 50 feet beyond, leads to the oxbow lake and then affords peeks of the Yellowstone River for 0.5 mile before the trail intersection at the upper end of Barbara's Slough. At this point, hikers can turn right and follow the bridle trail south of the slough back to their starting point at the bridge or, if the water is low, can cross and follow another trail east along the slough's north side back to the bridge.*

Ownership: DNR, managed by City of Billings (406) 657-8372
Size: 120 acres   **Closest Town:** Billings

Montana's largest carnivore is the grizzly bear, which can weigh as much as one thousand pounds. The smallest meat-eater is the least weasel, which tips the scales at less than two ounces.

69. POMPEYS PILLAR

Description: On the banks of the Yellowstone River, this good birding area is a mixture of cottonwoods, willows, and thickets, and includes a prominent sandstone bluff, Pompeys Pillar, named by William Clark of the Lewis and Clark expedition for Sacajawea's baby son. Clark signed his name and date on the bluff in 1806, and the site is now a Registered National Historic Landmark. Hike along the short trail or take the old road behind the visitor center and look for yellow warblers, northern flickers, and nuthatches in the cottonwoods and brush. At the river overlook, American white pelicans, great blue herons, Canada geese, and bald eagles frequently are seen. Around the bluff, watch for house and rock wrens, northern orioles, kestrels, turkey vultures, and prairie falcons. Yellow-bellied marmots are often seen on the pillar. The cultivated land adjacent to the bluff is owned by the BLM and managed by the FWP to improve wildlife habitat. Look for ring-necked pheasants, wild turkeys, red foxes, coyotes, and deer. In the fall, flocks of Canada geese can be seen feeding in the fields. There is also a small wetland and secondary river channel nearby that attracts waterfowl. The entire area is open to the public for hiking. Hikers should keep their eyes open for rattlesnakes, bull snakes, and garter snakes. Visitor center and parking lot open Memorial Day weekend through October 1; restrooms open year-round. Bird checklist, brochures available at visitor center. Hiking available year-round.

Directions: *From Billings, take Interstate 94 28 miles east to Exit 23. Follow the signs to the parking area and visitor center. The trailhead begins at the parking lot. If visiting during the off-season, park at the entrance gate and walk the 0.5 mile to the trailheads.*

Ownership: BLM (406) 657-6262
Size: 566 acres   **Closest Town:** Billings

70. HOWREY ISLAND

Description: A primitive, isolated Yellowstone River bottom area, Howrey Island is densely forested with cottonwoods and willows and dotted with small meadows. The island has a 1.3-mile self-guided trail with 10 marked stops. The island offers opportunities for birding; bald eagles, especially, are common in the summer with even larger populations in the winter. Red-tailed hawks, great horned owls, red-headed woodpeckers, warblers, great blue herons, and even wild turkeys have been spotted here. This part of the Yellowstone River is closed to waterfowl hunting, and concentrations of ducks and geese are often quite high. Wood ducks are common, and white-tailed deer are abundant. Also look for red foxes, beavers, and fox squirrels. Motorized access to the island is restricted. A brochure of the Howrey Island Nature Trail is available at the BLM offices in Miles City and Billings.

Directions: *Take Interstate 94 to Hysham, then follow Secondary Route 311 west for 6.9 miles to the Myers Bridge Fishing Access Site. Park here and walk to the island.*

Ownership: FWP; BLM (406) 232-7000
Size: 580 acres   **Closest Town:** Hysham

71. YELLOWTAIL DAM AFTERBAY

Description: This approximately 2-mile long body of water immediately below Yellowtail Dam is created by the much smaller afterbay dam. The water here seldom freezes, attracting an outstanding concentration of wintering waterfowl. Ducks and Canada geese can be seen most of the year, and thousands of birds arrive in the winter. As many as 47 bird species have been recorded here, commonly including green-winged teal, mallards, redheads, canvasbacks, ringnecks, Barrow's goldeneyes, hooded mergansers, grebes, and double-crested cormorants as well as oldsquaw (an ocean duck rarely seen in Montana). The afterbay and nearby portions of the Bighorn River may sustain as many as 20,000 wintering mallards. Avian predators include bald eagles in the winter (some nest nearby and can be seen all year), merlins, rough-legged hawks, prairie falcons, and an occasional peregrine falcon. Tundra swans, American white pelicans, common loons, and sandhill cranes may also appear during migration, as well as spotted sandpipers, killdeer, American avocets, and Wilson's phalaropes. There isn't much need for walking here—just bring binoculars and a spotting scope.

Directions: *From Hardin, take Secondary Route 313 to Fort Smith. The afterbay can be viewed from either the north side (cross the river at the afterbay dam) or the south side road and campground.*

Ownership: NPS (406) 666-2412
Size: 2-mile stretch of water　　**Closest Town:** Fort Smith

Birders flock to the area immediately below Yellowtail Dam in December and January to enjoy great views of wintering waterfowl, such as this Barrow's goldeneye.
ERWIN & PEGGY BAUER

72. BLACK'S POND DRIVE ROUTE

Description: Wildlife viewers who take this 23-mile Custer National Forest drive route will circle a timbered plateau that rises from the surrounding prairie. The ponderosa pine forest is interspersed with rugged breaks, creeks and ponds, and sagebrush flats. Black's Pond is a good place to see deer, wild turkeys, and songbirds. On the way in, the stream bottoms along Cow Creek and Stocker Branch Creek are good places to look for warblers, nuthatches, western tanagers, orioles, ovenbirds, solitary vireos, golden eagles, merlins, and kestrels. Near the junction of Forest Road 95 and Forest Road 131, watch for sharp-tailed grouse (there's a dancing ground near the junction of FR 95 and FR 794) and wild turkeys. Pronghorn are common on the open prairie, where mule and white-tailed deer are also present. Coyotes are seen frequently. Six bat species have been identified in the area, including the rare pallid bat; look for bats in the evening near Black's Pond, O'Dell Reservoir, and Cow Creek Reservoir. While there are no marked trails, hiking is possible almost anywhere. Bicycling and skiing are both good options in season. At Poker Jim Butte, a short distance off the drive route, there's a lookout with an exceptional view and a picnic area. A brochure describing the auto tour route and points of interest is available at all Custer National Forest offices. *DRIVE ROUTE IMPASSABLE NOVEMBER THROUGH APRIL; FOUR-WHEEL-DRIVE VEHICLE RECOMMENDED.*

Directions: *See map below. From Ashland, proceed east on U.S. Highway 212 for 3 miles, then follow Otter Creek Road (Secondary Route 484) south for 19 miles to Cow Creek Road (Forest Road 95). The drive route begins here. Follow Cow Creek Rd. for 5 miles, and from there take a loop trip. Turn right (north) onto Forest Road 131, travel 3 miles, and take Forest Road 3021 (Stocker Branch Road) to Black's Pond. Continue up FR 3021 about 2 miles and turn left (southwest) onto Forest Road 802. Go about 2 miles (past O'Dell Reservoir) and take a left on Forest Road 801. Follow this southeast for 2 miles, then take a left (east) and go back along Cow Creek Rd. (FR 95), which you follow back out to the Otter Creek Rd. (retracing the last 5 miles).*

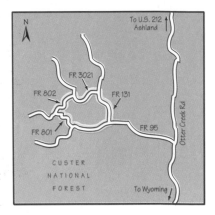

Ownership: USFS (406) 784-2344
Size: 44,800 acres; 23-mile drive
Closest Town: Ashland

 Most bats consume more than their weight in insects each night.

73. WM. L. MATTHEWS RECREATION & HABITAT MANAGEMENT AREA

Description: *URBAN SITE.*This exceptional riparian area along the Yellowstone River is covered with dense thickets of Russian olive, willow, and cottonwood trees, and has open meadows and fields. A short, paved loop trail leading from the parking lot provides barrier-free opportunities to view a variety of birds. In the spring and summer, look for American white pelicans, Canada geese, northern pintails, great blue herons, northern orioles, house wrens, red-tailed hawks, bald eagles, and wood ducks. In the fall, sandhill cranes and warblers can be seen on their migration. In the winter, long-eared owls, Canada geese, black-capped chickadees, robins, flickers, and mallards are present. Nearby fields and a shelterbelt hold ring-necked pheasants, red foxes, and white-tailed deer; skunks and raccoons commonly are seen. Another good birding site not far away is Pirogue Island Fishing Access Site, about 3 miles east of Miles City along the Yellowstone River. A float trip between Pirogue Island and Kinsey Bridge Fishing Access Site is a great way to see area wildlife.

Directions: *From Interstate 94 at Miles City, take old U.S. Highway 10 northeast approximately 10 miles. Take the Kinsey Road turnoff and proceed 0.25 mile to the site.*

Ownership: BLM (406) 232-7000
Size: 74 acres   **Closest Town:** Miles City

74. TERRY BADLANDS

Description: The Terry Badlands, immediately adjacent to the Yellowstone River, are rugged and beautiful. Deep chasms make walking difficult, but the bluffs, mixed grasses, juniper, and ponderosa pine provide great wildlife habitat. Racers, bull snakes, and rattlesnakes can be found here, and pronghorn, mule deer, coyotes, and red foxes often are seen. Golden eagles sometimes nest in the area and are seen frequently; other common nesting raptors include great horned owls and prairie falcons (look for cavities in the sandstone ledges). The raptors prey on the ever-abundant desert cottontails and white-tailed jackrabbits. Birds of special interest here include mockingbirds, Sprague's pipits, mountain plovers, long-billed curlews, and upland sandpipers. A walk along the bluffs on either side of the overlook offers opportunities to see piñon jays, western tanagers, and western meadowlarks. Hike in from the overlook or from the south along the old Milwaukee Road railroad grade. *DIRT ROAD IMPASSABLE WHEN WET.*

Directions: *Take Interstate 94 to Terry, then follow Secondary Route 253 north for about 2 miles. Turn left onto a dirt road and head west for 6 miles to a scenic overlook, or just park off the highway and walk.*

Ownership: BLM (406) 232-7000
Size: 43,000 acres   **Closest Town:** Terry

75. MAKOSHIKA STATE PARK

Description: Buttes, pinnacles, and spires that have eroded into fascinating shapes are features of this desolate badlands area. Although the climate is desertlike and the weather often extreme, the park hosts an impressive array of wildlife, including mule deer and coyotes. April 15 through October 15, as many as 50 turkey vultures can be seen in the park; look near Radio Hill and at the Buzzard Ridge view point. Golden eagles, American kestrels, prairie falcons, and red-tailed hawks can often be spotted circling overhead looking for prey. Look for Brewer's and vesper sparrows nesting in or under sagebrush. Other common birds are horned larks, western meadowlarks, mountain bluebirds, and lark sparrows. McCarty Pond and Spring is usually a good viewing area. Reptiles to look for include horned lizards (horned toads), bull snakes, and prairie rattle-snakes. For an excellent 0.6-mile walk through some unique geological features, take the Cap Rock Nature Trail—a good place to see rock wrens and turkey vultures. An auto tour booklet is available at the park visitor center, which also has numerous interpretive exhibits. *INQUIRE AT VISITOR CENTER FOR CURRENT ROAD CONDITIONS.*

Directions: *The park is 2 miles southeast of Glendive on Snyder Avenue; look for signs when entering town.*

Ownership: FWP (406) 365-6256
Size: 8,123 acres   **Closest Town:** Glendive

76. MEDICINE ROCKS STATE PARK

Description: The unique sandstone rock formations at this park are surrounded by prairie grasslands and ponderosa pine forests. President Teddy Roosevelt once described the area as "fantastically beautiful a place as I've ever seen." The park is an excellent place to see raptors of all kinds—red-tailed hawks, American kestrels, northern harriers, and ferruginous hawks. Golden eagles, merlins, prairie falcons, and cliff swallows nest on the cliffs. The prairie grasslands hold sharp-tailed grouse and a variety of songbirds, including the western meadowlark, mountain and eastern bluebird, rufous-sided towhee, and red-breasted nuthatch. A recent burn in the ponderosa pine forest has provided good habitat for woodpeckers. Mule deer and pronghorn are frequently seen. There is a large prairie dog town just west of the park (on private property, so look from afar), and red foxes and coyotes are sometimes seen hunting there. The Eagle Rock and Castle Rock areas are good for short walks. Look for horned lizards, bull snakes, and prairie rattlesnakes.

Directions: *From Baker, follow Montana Highway 7 south for 25 miles.*

Ownership: BLM, FWP (406) 232-4365
Size: 316 acres   **Closest Town:** Ekalaka

77. LONG PINES

Description: The ponderosa pine forests and aspen-lined draws at Long Pines are interspersed with sagebrush prairie and rocky, rolling hills. A fire burned much of this area in 1988, creating new wildlife habitat. Woodpeckers and bluebirds are especially abundant. It's a good place to see raptors, especially golden eagles and the nation's highest reported nesting density of merlins. Look for merlins hunting in the meadows and along the cliff edges—also good places to see great horned owls, American kestrels, and rough-legged hawks. Capitol Rock is an excellent place to look for golden eagles, while Abrogast Way Trail, a short distance to the northwest, is a good place to walk and see white-tailed deer. A few nearby springs host warblers and other songbirds. Long Pines birders should look for wild turkeys and a variety of songbirds; of special interest are ovenbirds and peewees. In the prairie areas look for rattlesnakes, bull snakes, and western meadowlarks. A tour route brochure is available at all Custer National Forest offices. *AREA HAS BOTH PUBLIC AND PRIVATE LANDS; PLEASE RESPECT THE RIGHTS OF PRIVATE LANDOWNERS. HIGH-CLEARANCE VEHICLES ONLY ON CAPITOL ROCK ROAD; FOUR-WHEEL-DRIVE VEHICLES ONLY DURING INCLEMENT WEATHER.*

Directions: *From Ekalaka, take Secondary Route 323 south 23 miles. Turn left (east) on the Tie Creek Road and follow it for 11.3 miles to Forest Road 118. Turn left (north) and drive 1 mile to the forest boundary—the beginning of the route. Follow this road north 3 miles to the junction of Forest Roads 117 and 118. Turn right (east) on FR 118 and follow it 1.4 miles to Capitol Rock Road. Turn right (south) on FR 117, or continue 6.2 miles east on FR 118 to the eastern boundary of the Long Pines Unit. Capitol Rock Rd. will exit the Long Pines Unit after 7 miles.*

Ownership: USFS (605) 797-4432
Size: 19,200 acres   **Closest Town:** Ekalaka

The distinctive cliffs of Medicine Rocks State Park provide nesting areas for eagles, hawks, and falcons, while the surrounding grasslands support sharp-tailed grouse, mule deer, coyotes, and numerous other species.   KRISTI DUBOIS

REGION SIX: MISSOURI RIVER COUNTRY

WILDLIFE VIEWING SITES

78. Little Rocky Mountains
79. Charles M. Russell NWR
80. Manning Corral Prairie Dog Town
81. UL Bend NWR
82. Bowdoin NWR
83. Bitter Creek
84. Missouri River, Downstream Recreation Area
85. The Pines Recreation Area
86. Jordan to Hell Creek Drive Route
87. Medicine Lake NWR
88. Fox Lake WMA
89. Elk Island

This land of high plains and badlands, native prairies, and forested coulees is the region where explorers Meriwether Lewis and William Clark vowed in their journals to speak no more of the abundant wildlife, for fear no one would believe them. Some of the largest tracts of prairie wilderness in the United States are found here, much of it within the boundaries of the Charles M. Russell and U.L. Bend national wildlife refuges. The spectacular wildlife viewing at Russell, second-largest refuge in the lower 48 states, includes prairie elk and bighorn sheep. U.L. Bend features one of the nation's largest prairie dog towns and a diversity of associated species: mountain plover, ferruginous hawk, burrowing owl, and badger, to name a few. The federally-listed endangered black-footed ferret has recently been reintroduced to this area. Bowdoin National Wildlife Refuge is a birder's paradise, with over 230 species identified.

78. LITTLE ROCKY MOUNTAINS

Description: The Little Rockies are heavily-timbered mountains that rise abruptly from the plains, providing habitat for a unique mix of mountain and prairie wildlife. Many species uncommon in eastern Montana are found here. The Camp Creek Campground is popular with birders—look for warblers, Clark's nutcrackers, and mountain chickadees. In the spring look for nesting prairie falcons on Silver Peak's southern cliffs, and golden eagles on the drive toward the mountains.See bighorn sheep (especially in winter) on the south side of Saddle Butte and Silver Peak as well as Lewis' woodpeckers and white-throated swifts. Look for blue grouse in Pony Gulch. Hike up Old Scraggy Peak from Beaver Creek to see mule and white-tailed deer, coyotes, beavers, and porcupines. Information and maps are available from the BLM office in Zortman (open June through August). *MINING AND LOGGING ROADS PROVIDE ACCESS; WATCH FOR TRUCKS AND HEAVY MACHINERY.*

Directions: *From Malta, take U.S. Highway 191 about 40 miles southwest, then follow a good county road towards Zortman for 7 miles, turning at the Camp Creek Campground turn-off.*

Ownership: Zortman Mining, Inc., Fort Belknap Indian Reservation, BLM (406) 654-1240

Size: 29,570 acres   **Closest Town:** Zortman

79. CHARLES M. RUSSELL NATIONAL WILDLIFE REFUGE TOUR ROUTE

Description: Passing through prairie grasslands, dense ponderosa pines, and thick sagebrush, with views of the scenic Missouri River, this is an exception car tour route. This second-largest refuge in the contiguous United States is probably the wildest remnant of the Northern Great Plains, with a full complement of prairie wildlife: mule and white-tailed deer, sharp-tailed grouse, prairie dogs, pronghorn, and many raptors. From mid-March through mid-May, view sharp-tailed grouse performing their unusual mating dances, about halfway through the route at post #10; in September, see and hear part of the nation's largest remaining prairie elk herd (nearly 4,000 animals) performing its fall mating rituals on the southern part of the tour along the Missouri River. No human entry is permitted in this section, but the elk can be easily seen and photographed from the road. Hiking is possible almost anywhere else. *GRAVEL ROAD MAY BE IMPASSABLE WHEN WET.*

Directions: *This approximately 2-hour, 20-mile auto tour route begins and ends on U.S. Highway 191. The north entrance is 55 miles from Malta; the south entrance is 0.5 mile north of where U.S. 191 crosses the Missouri.*

Ownership: USFWS (406) 538-8706

Size: 1.1 million acres Closest Towns: Lewistown, Malta

80. MANNING CORRAL PRAIRIE DOG TOWN

Description: Once an extensive black-tailed prairie dog town, located on the Charles M. Russell National Wildlife Refuge, this site is now a starkly beautiful prairie grassland dissected by steep gullies. The prairie colony contacted sylvatic plague in 1992 and experienced a large scale die-off. Prairie dogs are beginning to recolonize parts of the town, but recovery time is unknown. Prairie dogs have a complex social system that can be easily observed with binoculars. The town also attracts predators such as eagles, hawks, coyotes, bobcats, and badgers. It's a dependable place to see mountain plovers (midsummer is best). Mule deer and pronghorn are usually seen here as well. *ROADS IMPASSABLE WHEN WET.*

Directions: *See map, opposite page. From Malta, drive 44 miles south on U.S. Highway 191 to a dirt road heading east, immediately across the road from the Zortman turn-off. Take the right fork and follow the signs toward Lark Reservoir, then toward Gullwing Reservoir. Do not take the final turn-off to Gullwing; instead, proceed straight for about 1 mile to the refuge boundary and the dog town.*

Ownership: USFWS (406) 538-8706
Size: 1,000 acres   **Closest Town:** Zortman

81. UL BEND NATIONAL WILDLIFE REFUGE

Description: One of the nation's few prairie wilderness areas, this extremely remote refuge features native grasslands that give way to steep breaks overlooking the Missouri River. The area contains one of the highest densities of black-tailed prairie dog populations in the United States. The extensive dog towns attract coyotes, badgers, burrowing owls, golden eagles, ferruginous hawks, and during fall migration, merlins. This is one of the best spots in Montana to see mountain plovers. About 1.25 miles south of the refuge boundary on Refuge Road 212 is a display that interprets the prairie ecosystem. The Hawley Flat area (near Refuge Roads 319 and 219) is an excellent spot for the start of a walking tour. It's the site of a black-footed ferret (often called the nation's most endangered mammal) reintroduction, and one of the state's best places to find burrowing owls, as well as prairie rattlesnakes and elk. The Valentine Creek area (along Refuge Road 416) is a good spot to observe mating rituals of sage grouse in the spring. For dependable bighorn sheep viewing, take Refuge Road 418 to its end and hike up either Brandon Butte or Mickey Butte—-both are spectacular. Mountain bicycling is possible on much of UL Bend, but watch out for prickly pear cacti. *FOUR-WHEEL-DRIVE VEHICLES RECOMMENDED; ROADS IMPASSABLE WHEN WET*

Directions: *See map, opposite page. From Malta, follow U.S. Highway 191 south for 24 miles to Dry Fork Road, turn left, and drive east for 15 miles. Enter the refuge on Refuge Road 212, continue south for 1.5 miles, then turn east (left) onto Refuge Road 201 into the UL Bend area. A refuge map is needed; pick one up at administrative sites in Lewistown, Fort Peck, Sand Creek and Jordan.*

Ownership: USFWS (406) 538-8706
Size: 56,049 acres   **Closest Town:** Zortman, Malta

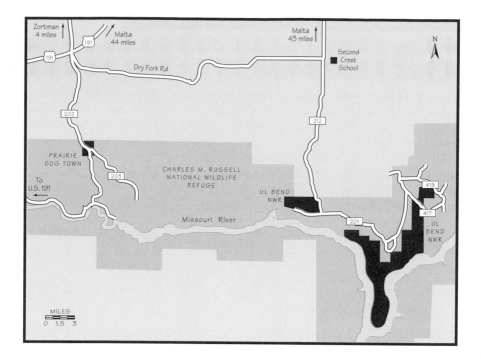

Although pronghorn populations were reduced to a few thousand in the 1920s, conservation efforts have spurred a rebound. Pronghorns in Montana today number more than 100,000. Most are found in the eastern half of the state, including such areas as the Charles M. Russell National Wildlife Refuge. MICHAEL S. SAMPLE

82. BOWDOIN NATIONAL WILDLIFE REFUGE

Description: The Bowdoin refuge consists mainly of shortgrass prairie, wetlands, scattered shelterbelts, and shrub fields. It offers exceptional viewing for waterfowl and more than 2,500 American white pelicans. See up to 50,000 ducks and geese during migration times. The refuge is especially known for its colonies of nesting birds—Franklin's gulls, black-crowned night herons, and white-faced ibis in the bulrush marshes, while American white pelicans, double-crested cormorants, and the California and ring-billed gulls occupy several islands. On Big Island (actually a peninsula), hike to see sharp-tailed grouse mating rituals in April and May (inquire at refuge headquarters). Common large mammals on the refuge include pronghorn, coyotes, and white-tailed deer. More than 236 bird species have been seen here, including notable species like Sprague's pipit and Baird's sparrow. Boating on main lake and Drumbo Unit only during fall hunting season. Leaflet on site shows auto tour. The tour route is open most times, but only during daylight hours in the fall. *ROAD IMPASSABLE WHEN WET.*

Directions: *From Malta, follow U.S. Highway 2 east for about 1 mile, then drive east on old U.S. 2 for about 6 miles.*

Ownership: USFWS (406) 654-2863
Size: 15,557 acres   **Closest Town:** Malta

83. BITTER CREEK

Description: Some of Montana's finest prairie wilderness, with both rugged badlands and open plains, can be found in this area. The eastern part of this large roadless area has occasional springs that foster the growth of cottonwood and aspen stands, which provide cover for white-tailed deer and a variety of songbirds. There are large winter concentrations of mule deer along the brushy draws, and pronghorn are abundant on the benches. Sharp-tailed grouse thrive on the buffaloberry in the brushy coulees, and sage grouse dwell in the silver sage of the benchlands. Several reservoirs have been constructed here, and have waterfowl nesting islands; Flat and Jug Reservoirs are both fairly accessible in the northern part of the area. Hiking is possible almost anywhere; walk through Eagle's Nest Coulee to see nesting prairie falcons and ferruginous hawks, as well as a prairie dog town that's just south of the coulee. *OFF-ROAD MOTORIZED TRAVEL PROHIBITED; ROADS IMPASSABLE WHEN WET.*

Directions: *Take U.S. Highway 2 about 5 miles east of Hinsdale, then turn north on Britsch Road and travel 14.9 miles to the beginning of the area. At mile 9.6, go straight on a less-traveled 2-track road. Stay on this road (keeping right) for 5.2 miles, then veer left. The Bitter Creek Wilderness Study Area sign marks the beginning of the area. A Bitter Creek brochure/map is available at the BLM office in Glasgow.*

Ownership: BLM (406) 228-4316
Size: 59,660 acres   **Closest Town:** Hinsdale

84. MISSOURI RIVER/DOWNSTREAM RECREATION AREA

Description: Below Fort Peck Reservoir is a remarkable mix of manmade ponds and natural habitats, including ponds, cottonwood bottoms, and willow thickets. During migration and winter, waterfowl and gulls are abundant on the ponds below the dam. Glaucous and Thayer's gulls are regular late fall and winter visitors, and 3 different species of loons have been seen here. Waterfowl include surf scoters, Barrow's goldeneyes, oldsquaws, snow geese, and wood ducks. Piping plovers are frequently seen near the reservoir by the dam. Look for migrating warblers on the Beaver Creek Nature Trail in Kiwanis Park. Bald eagle concentration in late fall. The Leo B. Coleman Wildlife Exhibit, just south of the dredge cuts, supports bison, elk, pronghorn, and deer. See sharp-tailed grouse mating rituals late March through May near Flat Lake; take Montana Highway 24 east from the dam and look for a sign to the lake.

Directions: *Directly below the Fort Peck power plants, reach the Missouri River by several roads. Reach the downstream area by turning north off Montana Highway 117 about 1 mile west of the plants. The dredge cuts are just north of Fort Peck along MT 117.*

Ownership: FWP, ACE, USFWS (406) 526-3464
Size: 1,205 acres   **Closest Town:** Fort Peck

85. THE PINES RECREATION AREA

Description: Beautiful ponderosa pines dot the rugged hills that dip into Fort Peck Reservoir at this site. A prairie elk herd numbers about 100 animals, mule deer are abundant, coyotes are common, and red foxes are occasionally seen. Common songbirds include mountain bluebirds, red-breasted nuthatches, black-capped chickadees, and during migration, a full range of warblers. Mudflats adjacent to the reservoir attract shorebirds, especially spotted sandpiper, marbled godwit, and greater and lesser yellowlegs. Nesting osprey are common, bald and golden eagle, prairie falcon, ferruginous hawk, and Swainson's hawk seen occasionally. Boat along the reservoir shore to see American white pelicans, gulls, and waterfowl. At dawn in the spring (April through May) view sage grouse mating rituals near the Pines area. Follow Willow Creek Road 4 miles past the Pines turnoff; look for grouse in the large cactus flat near the junction with TC access road. *ROADS MAY BE IMPASSABLE WHEN WET.*

Directions: *From Fort Peck, follow Montana Highway 24 north for about 5 miles to the Pines Recreation Area turnoff. Follow the signs; it's 26 miles of improved gravel road from the turnoff to the area.*

Ownership: ACE (406) 526-3411
Size: 1,080 acres   **Closest Town:** Fort Peck

86. JORDAN TO HELL CREEK DRIVE ROUTE

Description: Drive through sagebrush grasslands with deep draws and coulees on the way from Jordan to Hell Creek. In the early morning and late afternoon watch for wild turkeys near the road, as well as sage and sharp-tailed grouse, which mate in the spring (April through May). Look for a sage grouse lek in a sagebrush flat on the east side of the road after mile 12. Pronghorn, mule deer, and golden eagles are common. At the end of the road immediately adjacent to Fort Peck Reservoir, scattered ponderosa and limber pine shelter elk and songbirds (horned larks, thrashers, kingbirds, mountain bluebirds, vesper sparrows, piñon jays, western meadowlarks). In the bay along the reservoir it's easy to spot nesting osprey, American white pelicans, and Canada geese. During migration, it's a good place for viewing common loons.

Directions: *Take Montana Highway 200 to Jordan (milepost 213). Turn north on the county road and follow for 26 miles.*

Ownership: County, FWP (406) 232-4365
Size: 26-mile drive   **Closest Town:** Jordan

87. MEDICINE LAKE NATIONAL WILDLIFE REFUGE

Description: This remote refuge is one of the premier places in Montana to view and photograph birds and mammals. The area consists of rolling plains, small wetlands, shrublands, and a large lake with islands. As many as 100,000 ducks and geese migrate through, and more than 8,000 American white pelicans nest here, primarily on Big Island. Other islands have nesting populations of double-crested cormorants, great blue herons, California gulls, and ring-billed gulls. Thousands of sandhill cranes stopover in late October, and occasionally an endangered whooping crane. The courtship rituals of nesting grebes (both western and Clark's) provide exceptional spring viewing; watch them near where Montana Highway 16 crosses the west end of the lake. Look for piping plovers mid-May through early August along the gravel beaches on the east and south sides of Medicine and Gaffney Lakes. The refuge offers exceptional hiking, since nearly a third of it is designated wilderness. (The Sandhills area is especially good.) There's also outstanding canoeing (usually open except September 15 through November 15, but check at refuge headquarters; no motorboats allowed). An 18-mile auto tour from the refuge headquarters to Medicine Lake is open May 1 through September 30.

Directions: *From Wolf Point, drive east on U.S. Highway 2 for 47 miles to Culbertson. Turn north on Montana Highway 16, which runs through the west end of the refuge. The refuge headquarters is located on the northeast corner of the lake, 2 miles east of MT 16.*

Ownership: USFWS (406) 789-2305
Size: 31,457 acres   **Closest Town:** Medicine Lake

88. FOX LAKE WILDLIFE MANAGEMENT AREA

Description: A cattail and bulrush marsh located amid scenic rolling hills, this area is heavily used by waterfowl (up to 50,000 ducks and geese) and shorebirds for both nesting and resting during migration. There are 5 manmade nesting islands here, and dikes divide the lake into 10 independently regulated units. Breeding waterfowl include mallards, pintails, blue- and green-winged teal, shovelers, gadwalls, and redheads. Common shorebirds include American avocets, yellowlegs, willets, upland sandpipers, marbled godwits, and Wilson's phalaropes. Tundra swans and American white pelicans commonly visit, and sandhill cranes migrate through, especially in October. Sharp-tailed grouse, gray partridge, ring-necked pheasants, white-tailed and mule deer, pronghorn, and a variety of raptors can be seen in the upland habitat. Sprague's pipits and burrowing owls also have been seen here. Small boats are permitted in the marsh, and hiking is allowed anywhere; the best walking is along the top of the dikes. The area is open to hunting in the fall.

Directions: *Take Montana Highway 200 to Lambert, then follow a gravel county road south for 0.5 mile and turn right at the junction of 2 unnamed county roads. Continue for a little less than a mile to the Wildlife Management Area signs.*

Ownership: FWP (406) 228-9347
Size: 1,534 acres   **Closest Town:** Lambert

89. ELK ISLAND

Description: This Yellowstone River island and its associated riparian habitat supports one of the highest densities of white-tailed deer in Montana. There's fine birding for blue jays, waterfowl (especially wood ducks and Canada geese), wild turkeys, and pheasants. Fox squirrels, raccoons, and beavers are also common. Bald eagles may be seen in the spring and fall. Seasonally abundant are migrating warblers, American white pelicans, great blue herons, and woodpeckers. Freshwater mussels can be found along the river. Painted and snapping turtles are common. This is one of the few places in Montana where fireflies may be seen. The island is accessible only by boat, 0.75-mile downstream from the Elk Island Fishing Access. The river bottom is accessible to foot travel from the access road through the wildlife management area to the fishing access. There are no established trails, but plenty of wildlife paths to explore. A Yellowstone River float trip is also a good way to see area wildlife; put in at Intake, located 16 miles upriver, for a trip of approximately 18 miles; or put in at Elk Island and float 12 miles downstream to the Seven Sisters Fishing Access. Similar viewing opportunities exist at the Seven Sisters Wildlife Management Area east of Crane. All areas open to fall hunting.

Directions: *Take Montana Highway 16 to 0.5 mile north of Savage. Turn right onto County Road 344 and continue east, then north, for 1 mile. Turn right after crossing railroad tracks to enter WMA. Continue 1 mile along access road to reach the river.*

Ownership: FWP, BLM (406) 232-4365
Size: 1,276 acres (Elk Island); 696 acres (Seven Sisters)
Closest Town: Savage

REGION SEVEN: GLACIER NATIONAL PARK

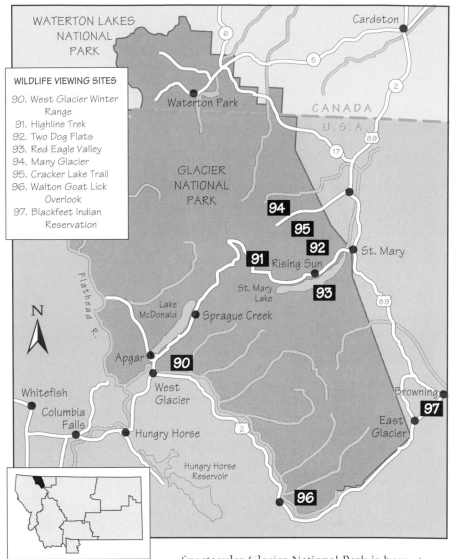

WATERTON LAKES
NATIONAL
PARK

WILDLIFE VIEWING SITES
90. West Glacier Winter
    Range
91. Highline Trek
92. Two Dog Flats
93. Red Eagle Valley
94. Many Glacier
95. Cracker Lake Trail
96. Walton Goat Lick
    Overlook
97. Blackfeet Indian
    Reservation

Cardston

Waterton Park

CANADA
U.S.A.

GLACIER
NATIONAL
PARK

94

95

92

St. Mary

91 Rising Sun

St. Mary
Lake

93

Flathead R.

N

Lake
McDonald

Sprague Creek

Apgar

90

West
Glacier

Whitefish

Columbia
Falls

Hungry Horse

Hungry Horse
Reservoir

Browning

97

East
Glacier

96

Spectacular Glacier National Park is home to 60 native mammal species, over 200 bird species, 5 amphibian species, and 2 varieties of nonvenomous snakes. In summer, the Logan Pass area offers excellent wildlife viewing, especially near Hidden Lake or along the Highline Trail. In spring and fall, the prairie grasslands east of the Continental Divide near St. Mary are home to raptors, songbirds, herds of elk, and a bounty of wildflowers. Glacier's lower-elevation areas, windblown clearings, and south-facing slopes become wildlife havens during the long winter. One of the great privileges of a visit to this pristine park is the chance to observe free-roaming wildlife in its natural habitats. Visitors can make it a project to sharpen their powers of observation, noting the behavior of animals and their selection of natural foods without disturbance from people.

90. WEST GLACIER WINTER RANGE

Description: Elk, white-tailed deer, and mule deer congregate in this area on the Park's southern boundary along U.S. Highway 2, the site of an old burn. The best viewing time is late fall through winter on south-facing slopes. An occasional coyote can be spotted and bald eagles can sometimes be seen along the Middle Fork of the Flathead River; binoculars or spotting scopes are recommended. A trail on the Park side of the river (reached by crossing the old bridge near West Glacier) is a nice 2- to 3-mile walk or cross-country ski trip into the winter range. Winter is a stressful time for wildlife, so view from a distance.

Directions: *From West Glacier, drive approximately 3 miles east and watch for range viewing signs.*

Size: 8,500 acres

The gray wolf has been naturally recolonizing northwestern Montana for most of the last decade. Wolves currently are being reintroduced in Yellowstone National Park.
WILLIAM MUNOZ

GLACIER NATIONAL PARK

91. HIGHLINE TREK

Description: Hikers who take this 7.6-mile route to Granite Park Chalet will see an outstanding panorama of the Park. In the high alpine meadows, watch for bighorn sheep, marmots, and mountain goats. The goats and sheep are often seen on mountainsides 3 miles into the trail near Haystack Butte. Rosy finches, golden eagles, mountain bluebirds, and water pipits also can be seen along the way. The Granite Park Chalet terrace is one of the continent's best places to safely view grizzly bears; it overlooks the spectacular Bear Valley, which is heavily used by bears and closed to humans. Golden eagles are sometimes seen, especially in the autumn, and pikas are often seen and heard on the trail.

Directions: *The trail begins at the Logan Pass Visitor Center. Park in the large lot, then cross Going-to-the-Sun Road and hike along the Continental Divide (heading northwest) for 7.6 miles to Granite Park Chalet.*

Size: 7.6-mile hike

92. TWO DOG FLATS

Description: Spring and early summer wildflowers such as Indian paintbrush, lupine, and blanketflower are abundant in this open prairie. Visitors may see prairie falcons and other raptors, a variety of songbirds (including white-crowned sparrows and MacGillivray's warblers), ground squirrels, and coyotes. Elk are seen at dawn and dusk, particularly in the spring and fall.

Directions: *From the St. Mary Visitor Center, travel west for 4 miles along Going-to-the-Sun Road.*

Size: 500 acres

Glacier National Park is one of the best places to see the white-tailed ptarmigan, a bird of high peaks and alpine tundra. Ptarmigan blend into their surrounding habitat by molting—their feathers are stark white in winter, then mottled brown in summer. This phenomenon is known as protective coloration.
MICHAEL S. SAMPLE

93. RED EAGLE VALLEY

Description: The trail to Red Eagle Lake passes through coniferous forests, open grasslands, and aspen and cottonwood groves. It's an excellent site for birders to walk, for just a mile or all the way to the lake. The cottonwood groves and grasslands are good places to see chipping sparrows, yellow warblers, Swainson's thrushes, and red-naped sapsuckers. The mountain meadows and old-growth spruce forests are good spots to look for northern three-toed woodpeckers, tree swallows, and golden-crowned kinglets. Beavers inhabit the ponds near brushy areas. Those who hike all the way to Red Eagle Lake may see a common loon or moose there. Red Eagle Mountain is a good place to view mountain goats; use binoculars to scan the peak. This trail is also good for cross-country skiing when there's snow; designated ski loops stay within 3 miles of the trailhead and travel through elk winter range. Be wary of frequent mountain lion travel; visitors are advised to make noise, especially on windy days or around running water.

Directions: *In St. Mary, go to the 1913 Ranger Station where the Red Eagle Trailhead begins. Hike 7 miles to Red Eagle Lake.*

Size: 7-mile trail

94. MANY GLACIER

Description: Wildlife is abundant in the Many Glacier area. On the drive in, watch for bald eagles along Sherburne Reservoir. Look for bears and coyotes in the aspen groves; listen for common loons and bugling elk in the fall. A number of hiking trails in the valley lead to high country lakes and glaciers where wildlife can be seen. Mountain goats are common on Grinnell Point, while bighorn sheep are often seen near Ptarmigan Lake. Grizzly bears are often seen on the talus slopes along the upper part of Mount Altyn. In November, bighorn sheep move to lower elevations and are sometimes visible, particularly on the lower slopes of Mount Altyn.

Directions: *Take U.S. Highway 89 to Babb, then drive 12 miles west into the Many Glacier Valley.*

Size: 64,000 acres

Even though riparian areas make up less than one-half of one per cent of Montana's land area, fully one-half of the state's bird species nest only in these streamside areas.

GLACIER NATIONAL PARK

Mountain goats are frequently seen by hikers on the Hidden Lake Trail from Logan Pass. This male, or "billy," surveys his rocky domain above Hidden Lake.
MICHAEL S. SAMPLE

95. CRACKER LAKE TRAIL

Description: The aspen stands, conifers, open grasslands, and old-growth forests along this trail support a diversity of life. Make some noise while walking, especially on windy days and around running water, since this area is heavily used by grizzly bears. Rufous and calliope hummingbirds, common yellowthroats, olive-sided flycatchers, and sharp-shinned hawks can be seen along the trail, as well as an occasional prairie falcon or golden eagle. Northern hawk owls (large diurnal owls) may be seen hunting or perched on the lower branches of a spruce tree. Hoary marmots and Columbian ground squirrels are common. The steep slopes of Allen Mountain near the lake are a very good place to see bighorn sheep and mountain goats; use binoculars.

Directions: *From Babb, drive 5 miles west to Many Glacier. The trailhead begins at the Many Glacier Hotel parking lot.*

Size: 6-mile trail

96. WALTON GOAT LICK OVERLOOK

Description: This lush and beautiful area is a great place to see mountain goats. The best goat viewing takes place April through early July at the natural mineral-laden cliffs adjacent to the Middle Fork of the Flathead River. As many as 20 goats may be viewed at a time browsing on vegetation on the wind-swept slopes adjacent to the road. Deer, and especially elk, are often visible on the roadside near this natural mineral deposit.

Directions: *Take U.S. Highway 2 about 2 miles southeast of Essex. The parking area down by the river is closed in the winter, but there is still ample space to pull over on the roadside. The overlook is adjacent to the road.*

Size: 200 acres

GLACIER NATIONAL PARK

A bald eagle's wings can spread wider than most humans are tall. Its keen eyes may spot another eagle soaring over 30 miles away. An eagle may strike its prey with twice the impact of a bullet.

Description: This 12-mile drive route along the Blackfeet Indian Reservation is dotted by thousands of prairie pothole wetlands that are rare in the state and becoming rarer. These potholes were left behind following the retreat of glaciers and contain prime grasslands with many wildlife species. The reservation wetlands are used by numerous species of waterfowl and raptors. Golden eagles frequently are seen along the roadside, surveying the pothole activity (particularly in the spring and fall). Also look for migrating snow geese, and tundra and trumpeter swans. Breeding waterfowl here include mallards, northern shovelers, gadwalls, pintails, American widgeons, and canvasbacks. Shorebirds include American avocets and piping plovers.

Directions: *The 12-mile drive route along U.S. Highway 2 starts at East Glacier and ends at Browning. Potholes are located throughout the 12-mile stretch on either side of the road. Parking is limited, so drive slowly and look for pullouts along the route.*

Ownership: Blackfeet Tribe (406) 338-7207
Size: 12-mile drive

FIELD TECHNIQUES AND CAUTIONS FOR
WILDLIFE VIEWERS IN GLACIER NATIONAL PARK

Viewing wildlife in Glacier National Park can be a thrilling experience for visitors. However, as visitation increases, so do pressures on wildlife. The following recommendations will help to minimize the stress that wildlife may feel.

• Don't photograph or view wildlife from a close range. Use binoculars for viewing and a telephoto lens for photographing. Winter and spring are especially stressful times for mountain dwellers, when crucial reserves may be depleted because of unwanted disturbances. If an animal changes its behavior because of you, you're too close.
• Interference during mating and rearing young may result in abandonment or inadvertent separation of mates or of adults from their young. Restrict your activities around bird nests and avoid approaching animals with young.
• Feeding wildlife is prohibited in Glacier National Park and violators are subject to a large fine. A FED BEAR IS A DEAD BEAR. Habituated bears—bears that have received positive reinforcement in the form of food—will be destroyed. Feeding wild animals is dangerous and may have unhealthy consequences or fatal results for the animals. Animals such as Columbian ground squirrels naturally develop yellow fat cells as they gain weight for their hibernation. However, human food can cause them to develop white fat cells, and they may die in their burrows without enough fat reserves to sustain them through the winter.

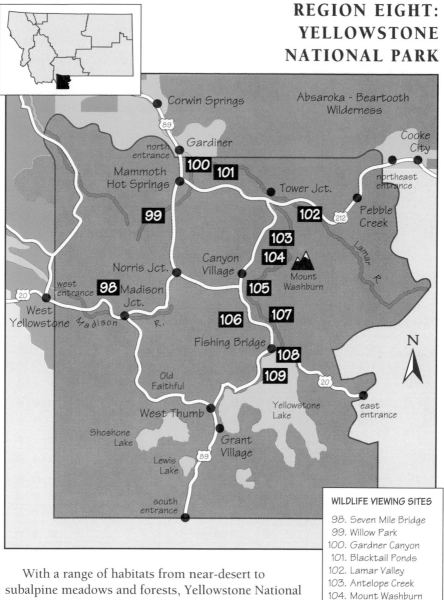

Corwin Springs

Absaroka - Beartooth
Wilderness

89

Gardiner

north
entrance

Cooke
City

Mammoth
Hot Springs

100 **101**

northeast
entrance

Tower Jct.

99

102 212

Pebble
Creek

Lamar R.

103

104

Canyon
Village

Mount
Washburn

Norris Jct.

west
entrance

98 Madison
Jct.

20

105

West
Yellowstone

Madison R.

106 **107**

Fishing Bridge

108

Old
Faithful

109

20

N

West Thumb

Yellowstone
Lake

east
entrance

Shoshone
Lake

Grant
Village

Lewis
Lake

89

south
entrance

WILDLIFE VIEWING SITES

98. Seven Mile Bridge
99. Willow Park
100. Gardner Canyon
101. Blacktail Ponds
102. Lamar Valley
103. Antelope Creek
104. Mount Washburn
105. Grand Canyon of
   the Yellowstone
106. Hayden Valley
107. LeHardy Rapids
108. Fishing Bridge
109. Yellowstone Lake

With a range of habitats from near-desert to subalpine meadows and forests, Yellowstone National Park is home to a variety and abundance of wildlife unparalleled in the lower 48 states. Nearly all wildlife species inhabiting the park when it was first explored more than 100 years ago survive today. Wildlife viewing success here depends on knowledge of particular species—their habitat preferences, seasonal movements, and geographic distribution. The viewing chart on the following page offers a quick cross-reference of selected species and their typical haunts during the summer.

SUMMER WILDLIFE VIEWING IN YELLOWSTONE NATIONAL PARK

The animals of Yellowstone are more dispersed in the summer and are found in every habitat type in the park, from the highest elevations to the lowest. During the summer months, the Yellowstone Plateau has the greatest variety and abundance of wildlife. The following chart provides at-a-glance information for viewing selected species during summer.

Viewing Areas	Coyote	Grizzly bear	Black bear	Moose	Elk	Bison	Mule deer	Bighorn sheep	Pronghorn	Fish	Trumpeter swan	Bald eagle	Peregrine falcon	Osprey	American white pelican	Sandhill crane	Waterbirds, various	Songbirds, various
Fountain Flats	●				●	●										●	●	●
Seven Mile Bridge	●				●	●					●	●		●			●	●
National Park Meadow	●				●	●						●	●			●	●	●
Gibbon Meadow	●				●	●							●				●	●
Norris Meadow	●				●	●											●	●
Willow Park				●	●											●		●
Swan Lake Flats	●	●			●	●			●		●					●	●	●
Mammoth Hot Springs	●		●		●	●	●		●					●			●	●
Gardner Canyon	●				●		●	●	●			●		●			●	●
Gardiner	●				●	●	●		●					●				●
Blacktail Ponds			●		●	●										●	●	●
Floating Island Lake	●	●	●		●		●		●								●	●
Lamar Valley	●	●		●	●	●	●		●			●	●			●	●	●
Antelope Creek	●	●		●	●	●			●							●		●
Mount Washburn Trail					●			●										●
Grand Canyon of the Yellowstone													●	●				●
Hayden Valley	●	●		●	●	●					●	●	●	●	●	●	●	●
LeHardy Rapids										●				●				●
Fishing Bridge	●	●		●	●					●		●			●	●	●	●
Mary Bay	●	●			●	●								●			●	●
Lewis River				●													●	●

FIELD TECHNIQUES AND CAUTIONS FOR WILDLIFE VIEWERS IN YELLOWSTONE NATIONAL PARK

• Contrary to what you may have been told, bears are everywhere in Yellowstone. Bears may be seen reliably from the park's roadsides, with binoculars and spotting scopes. If you decide to hike, always be alert and pay attention to your surroundings. For the safest hiking in bear country, always travel in groups of 4 or more.

• DO NOT APPROACH BEARS! Both grizzly and black bears are unpredictable, making them extremely dangerous. Park visitors have been seriously injured, maimed, and, in some cases, killed by bears.

• Odors attract bears. Never leave food or garbage unattended. Dispose of garbage in bear-proof waste containers. If camping, store all food and cooking gear in a secure place, such as the trunk of a car, or suspended 10 feet above the ground and 4 feet out from a tree trunk or post. Selected campsites in the park offer food storage boxes.

• Bison are much more dangerous than they appear. Each year visitors are injured by bison; two visitors have been killed to date. Bison may charge without giving a behavioral warning. Individual bison may weigh as much as one ton, and can quickly reach speeds of 30 miles per hour. Keep at least 50 yards from bison at all times, and always have an escape route in mind. The best rule of thumb is to remain close to your vehicle.

• DO NOT FEED WILDLIFE UNDER ANY CONDITIONS. Visitors who feed wild animals only prove their ignorance and disregard for Yellowstone's wildlife. Animals fed by humans will lose their fear of people and become more vulnerable to predators. They may also become reliant on handouts and fail to maintain their own feeding habits. Feeding wildlife can lead to a $50 fine.

• Use binoculars or spotting scopes to get close to wildlife. This is the best way to observe the natural activities of animals without disrupting their behavior. Photographers interested in getting close-up shots of wildlife should use large telephoto lenses.

• The best way to view wildlife is from a vehicle. Wildlife are accustomed to vehicles along roadways. Your car is the perfect observation blind.

• Early morning and evening are the prime hours for wildlife viewing.

• The use of playback recorders is illegal in Yellowstone National Park; violaters face a $100 fine.

• Traffic delays are a way of life in Yellowstone during the summer. Drive defensively and please be patient.

98. SEVEN MILE BRIDGE

Description: This bridge is the most reliable place in Yellowstone for viewing trumpeter swans, which nest in the vicinity; listen for their low-pitched trumpetlike call. *DO NOT FEED THE SWANS*; Artificial feeding of these birds only contributes to their deaths in the long run. Osprey, mallards, green-winged teal, Canada geese, tree swallows, barn swallows, and sandhill cranes can often be found here in the summer. In the winter, swans congregate here, as do bison and bald eagles. Elk can be heard bugling in nearby meadows in the fall.

Directions: *The bridge is 7 miles east of West Yellowstone, and halfway between Madison Junction and the Park's West Entrance.*

Size: 320 acres

99. WILLOW PARK

Description: Watch for moose browsing on willows (their preferred food) here, especially at dawn and dusk in the summer. Moose are seldom seen at Willow Park in the winter; instead they occupy areas of old-growth timber where they are sheltered from the elements and have access to browse plants. In the summer, the willow stands provide good habitat for a variety of songbirds—Wilson's warblers, yellow warblers, Lincoln's sparrows, and common yellowthroats. In the lodgepole pine forest surrounding the meadow look for yellow-rumped warblers, dark-eyed juncos, hairy woodpeckers, and red-breasted nuthatches.

Directions: *From Mammoth Hot Springs, drive about 10 miles south toward Norris. The Willow Park site is between Apollinaris Spring and Indian Creek Campground.*

Size: 1,920 acres

100. GARDNER CANYON

Description: Home to an abundance of wildlife, this canyon is an excellent place to see bighorn sheep and pronghorn year-round (especially in the winter), and mule deer and elk in the fall, winter, and spring. In the summer, it is also one of the best places in the park to look for colorful songbirds, including lazuli buntings, western tanagers, and green-tailed towhees. Other birds to watch for in the summer are golden eagles, red-tailed hawks, Clark's nutcrackers, and prairie falcons. Cliff swallows make their homes on the surrounding canyon walls. In the winter, watch for Townsend's solitaires and look for American dippers bobbing up and down on rocks in the Gardner River. Winter bighorn sheep viewing is exceptional at McMinn Bench east of the canyon; 2 access points, one north and one south of the canyon, lead to McMinn Bench. The canyon proper and cliffs are closed to the public to prevent rock fall and allow a safe haven for sheep.

Directions: *Enter the Park from the North Entrance at Gardiner and drive to either the Rescue Creek Bridge or the 45th Parallel parking areas.*

Size: 2,560 acres

101. BLACKTAIL PONDS

Description: These ponds come alive with birdlife in the spring. The Blacktail Ponds (4 connected ponds of Blacktail Creek) are among the first to thaw in the spring, attracting red-winged blackbirds, lesser scaup, American coots, yellow-headed blackbirds, sandhill cranes, soras, and common snipes. Floating Island Lake (8 miles east of Blacktail Ponds) offers outstanding birding opportunities as well, with a similar complement of birdlife.

Directions: *The Blacktail Ponds are 6.6 miles east of Mammoth Hot Springs en route to Tower Junction.*

Size: 8.8 acres

102. LAMAR VALLEY

Description: The expansive landscapes of the Lamar Valley are home to huge herds of elk and bison, particularly in the winter. Coyotes abound in this area year-round, searching for ungulate carcasses and rodents. Grizzly and black bears can be viewed in the area in the spring and summer, particularly south of the Yellowstone Institute (at the Lamar Valley Ranger Station). In the summer, look for mule deer, pronghorn, and an occasional badger. Golden eagles, red-tailed hawks, prairie falcons, and American kestrels frequent the valley's long, expansive meadow. Just 1.5 miles east of the confluence of Soda Butte Creek and the Lamar River is a trailhead. The trail goes upriver and offers good cross-country skiing and beautiful scenic views.

Directions: *Enter the Park from the North Entrance at Gardiner or the Northeast Entrance near Cooke City. The Lamar Valley lies midway between Tower Junction and the Northeast Entrance.*

Size: 70,000 acres

Wildlife watching includes small, common animals, such as this least chipmunk, one of the most-viewed creatures by visitors to Yellowstone National Park. Feeding these small animals can make them accustomed to people and more vulnerable to predation.
MICHAEL S. SAMPLE

103. ANTELOPE CREEK

Description: With a good pair of binoculars, a spotting scope, and some patience, this is one of the most reliable places to safely view grizzly bears in Yellowstone. The best viewing times are dawn and dusk. In June grizzlies traditionally stalk elk calves in this basin, although bears can be seen here May through October. The Antelope Creek area is closed to human entry for safety reasons; all viewing is strictly from the road. Several good pullouts offer unobstructed views. Just north of Tower Falls, look for bighorn sheep on the steep cliffs east of the road. Red-tailed hawks are also found in this area.

Directions: *From Tower Junction, drive just a few miles south past Tower Falls. Stop at any of the pullouts and glass the hillsides.*

Size: 3,200 acres

104. MOUNT WASHBURN

Description: A hike up Mount Washburn passes through alpine tundra and provides panoramas of wild country. In the summer, bighorn sheep can be seen on the mountain. Hikers may encounter blue grouse on the way, or red squirrels harvesting whitebark pine cones; the nuts from the cones are a major food of Yellowstone grizzly bears, particularly in the fall. Noisy Clark's nutcrackers also pick and store the nuts for winter; the seeds they don't find become tomorrow's whitebark pines. Other summer birds here include hairy woodpeckers, prairie falcons, golden eagles, peregrine falcons, gray jays, and occasionally rosy finches. This is fragile alpine tundra, so please do not leave the trail. *THIS 6-MILE ROUND-TRIP HIKE TAKES 3 HOURS AND CLIMBS 1,400 VERTICAL FEET. BE SURE TO CARRY WATER.*

Directions: *Mount Washburn is accessible via a 3-mile hike from 2 points on the Tower-Canyon road. Either park at the Dunraven Pass picnic area or drive 1 mile up the old Chittenden Road (4 miles north of Dunraven Pass) to a parking area.*

Size: 3-mile hike
(to an altitude of 10,243 feet)

105. GRAND CANYON OF THE YELLOWSTONE

Description: This spectacular canyon is a great area for viewing nesting raptors. It's probably the best place in the park to see osprey; as many as 7 nesting pairs can be seen and a nest can almost always be spotted by searching the rock pinnacles. (Ask a ranger if you can't find one.) Look for nesting osprey mid-June through early July on the canyon's rocky pinnacles. Also watch for American kestrels, Clark's nutcrackers, common ravens, and gray jays.

Directions: *At Canyon Junction take North Rim Drive east to Grandview and Lookout Point.*

Size: 6,400 acres

The Grand Canyon of the Yellowstone River is one of the most spectacular scenes in Yellowstone National Park. Look for nesting ospreys along this area during the summer.   JOHN REDDY

106. HAYDEN VALLEY

Description: The Hayden Valley may well be Yellowstone's most spectacular wildlife area. Look for grizzly bears digging for pocket gophers in spring and bellowing bison breeding in summer (late July through early August); watch for bison uncovering grass from deep snow with swings of their massive heads in winter. The Alum Creek pullout is a good place to look for shorebirds, including long-billed dowitchers, western sandpipers, and greater yellowlegs in the spring and fall. The Yellowstone River holds American white pelicans, trumpeter swans, Canada geese, Barrow's goldeneyes, and mallards. Look for sandhill cranes and coyotes in the open meadows. This is a great place to listen for bugling elk in the fall.

Directions: *The Hayden Valley is a large open meadow lying between Canyon and Fishing Bridge. There are many pullouts and overlooks, so don't obstruct traffic.*

Size: 18,000 acres

Grizzly bears are sometimes seen along Antelope Creek in Yellowstone National Park. These animals are the largest carnivores in Montana, though in fact a Yellowstone grizzly's diet is usually 60 percent plants and 40 percent meat. Grizzly bears in Yellowstone often prey on elk calves in the spring. Be sure to make noise while hiking on trails in grizzly country to avoid a too-close encounter. TOM MANGELSEN

107. LEHARDY RAPIDS

Description: During June and July at this site, watch spawning cutthroat trout leap the rapids, then rest in pools just below them. Rare harlequin ducks are sometimes seen diving into the turbulent water, looking for aquatic insects. This is also a good spot to see American dippers and an occasional river otter. Gray jays can be seen in the nearby conifers. *FISHING PROHIBITED WITHIN 100 YARDS OF EITHER SIDE OF RAPIDS.*

Directions: *The rapids are halfway between Mud Volcano (south of Canyon Village) and Fishing Bridge on the east side of the road.*

Size: 50 acres

108. FISHING BRIDGE

Description: Watch native cutthroat trout spawn under this famous bridge in June and July. American white pelicans can sometimes be seen catching fish in the shallow waters, swallowing their catch whole. Barrow's goldeneyes and California gulls are commonly seen here. Watch for coyotes walking along the shore and searching for food.

Directions: *Fishing Bridge is at the north end of Yellowstone Lake.*

Size: 50-yard-long bridge

109. YELLOWSTONE LAKE

Description: Take a 1-hour boat tour around Stevenson Island for an outstanding opportunity to view bald eagles. (The island is closed to the public May 15 through August 15 to protect nesting birds.) Look for California gulls, buffleheads, and Barrow's goldeneyes near Bridge Bay and watch for gray jays and Clark's nutcrackers in forested areas along the shoreline. Yellowstone Lake is large, deep, and cold, so small boats should stay close to shore; stay off the lake during windy weather. Boat tours run June 4 through September 17; the cost is under $10 for adults and under $5 for children (ages 5 to 11). Gull Point Drive, along the shoreline just south of Bridge Bay, is a good area to look for belted kingfishers, lesser scaup, buffleheads, and spotted sandpipers.

Directions: *From Bridge Bay Marina, take a short boat tour around Stevenson Island, or use your own boat to discover the lake.*

Size: 91,704 acres

WILDLIFE INDEX

This index features unusual or sought-after wildlife species, and the best sites for viewing them. Many species identified below may be seen at other sites as well. The numbers following each listing refers to the site number, not the page number.

SUGGESTED READING

The Birder's Guide to Montana, Terry McEneaney, Falcon Press, 1993.

The Field Guide to Wildlife Habitats of the Western U.S., Janine M. Benyus, Simon and Shuster, 1989.

For Everything There is a Season: The Sequence of Natural Events in the Grand Teton-Yellowstone Area, Frank C. Craighead, Jr., Falcon Press, 1994.

A Guide to Animal Tracking and Behavior, Donald and Lillian Stokes, Little, Brown and Company, 1986.

Montana, Norma Tirrell, Compass American Guides, 1991.

Small Mammals of the Yellowstone Ecosystem, Donald Streubel, Roberts Rinehart, 1989.

WHERE THE WILD THINGS ARE

Falcon Press puts wildlife viewing secrets at your fingertips with our high-quality, full color guidebooks—the Watchable Wildlife series. This is the only official series of guides for the National Watchable Wildlife Program: areas featured in the books correspond to official sites across America. And you'll find more than just wildlife. Many sites boast beautiful scenery, interpretive displays, opportunities for hiking, picnics, biking, plus—a little peace and quiet. So pick up one of our Wildlife Viewing Guides today and get close to Mother Nature!

WATCH THIS PARTNERSHIP WORK

The National Watchable Wildlife Program was formed with one goal in mind: get people actively involved in wildlife appreciation and conservation. Defenders of Wildlife has led the way by coordinating this unique multi-agency program and developing a national network of prime wildlife viewing areas.

FALCON